203

D0329251

THE COMPLETE BOOK OF
COLLECTING ART NOUVEAU

John Mebane

THE COMPLETE BOOK

OF

Collecting Art Nouveau

WEATHERVANE BOOKS • NEW YORK

Copyright © MCMLXX by John Mehane
Library of Congress Catalog Card Number: 76-132618
All rights reserved.
This edition is published by Weathervane Books
a division of Imprint Society, Inc., distributed by Crown Publishers, Inc.
by arrangement with Coward McCann, Inc.
a b c d e f g h
Manufactured in the United States of America

Acknowledgments

The AUTHOR is indebted to several individuals, museums, and institutions for helping make this book possible through the provision of illustrative materials and other assistance.

These include: Mr. Sy Baron and the Incurable Collector of Montreal, Canada; Mrs. Louise Ade Boger of New York City; Mr. and Mrs. Mike D. Cole, Marietta, Georgia; the Corning Museum of Glass, Corning Glass Center, Corning, New York; the Gorham Company, Providence, Rhode Island; Mr. Clarence T. Hubbard, West Hartford, Connecticut; Mr. E. P. Hogan, Historical Librarian, and the International Silver Company, Meriden, Connecticut; the Metropolitan Museum of Art, New York; Musée des Arts Décoratifs, Paris; the Museum of Modern Art, New York City; Mr. and Mrs. C. C. Pritchard and the Golden Peacock, St. Augustine, Florida; the Lightner Municipal Exposition, St. Augustine, Florida; Mrs. Katharine Morrison McClinton, New York City; and the Victoria and Albert Museum, London.

For permission to quote from works published by them, the author expresses his appreciation of the following publishers and individuals: Harry N. Abrams, Inc., New York City, publisher of *Art Nouveau* by Robert Schmutzler; Mrs. Dorothy McGraw Bogue, Colorado Springs, Colorado, author of *The Van Briggle Story;* Mrs. Peggy Joyce Gurn, co-author with William E. Mouser, Jr., of *Cristal d'Émile Gallé;* the

5

Mid-America Book Company of Leon, Iowa, publishers of *Zanesville Art Pottery in Color* by Louise and Evan Purviance and Norris F. Schneider; the Museum of Modern Art, New York City, publishers of *Art Nouveau and Design at the Turn of the Century* edited by Peter Selz and Mildred Constantine (distributed by Doubleday & Company, Inc., Garden City, New York); Thomas Nelson, Inc., Camden, New Jersey, publishers of *American Art Nouveau Glass* by Albert Christian Revi; Praeger Publishers, New York City, publishers of *The Sources of Modern Architecture and Design* by Nikolaus Pevsner; and George Wittenborn, Inc., New York City, publishers of *Sources of Art Nouveau* by Stephan Tschudi Madsen. He also expresses appreciation to *The Antiques Journal,* for permission to quote from an article by Mr. Clarence T. Hubbard appearing in this publication.

Contents

Introduction   9

I   *Identifying Art Nouveau*   15

II   *Art Nouveau Glass*   27

III   *Art Nouveau Pottery*   53

IV   *Art Nouveau Jewelry*   71

V   *Art Nouveau Silver*   91

VI   *Clocks, Watches, and Their Accessories*   109

VII   *Of Special Feminine Interest*   119

VIII   *Of Special Interest to Men*   133

IX   *Writing Accessories*   147

X   *Miscellaneous Table Accessories*   159

XI   *Candlesticks and Candelabra*   171

XII   *Art Nouveau Furniture*   179

XIII   *Graphic Arts and Sculpture*   195

XIV   *What About Prices?*   211

XV   *On the Trail of the Prize*   239

Selected Bibliography   247

Notes   251

Index   253

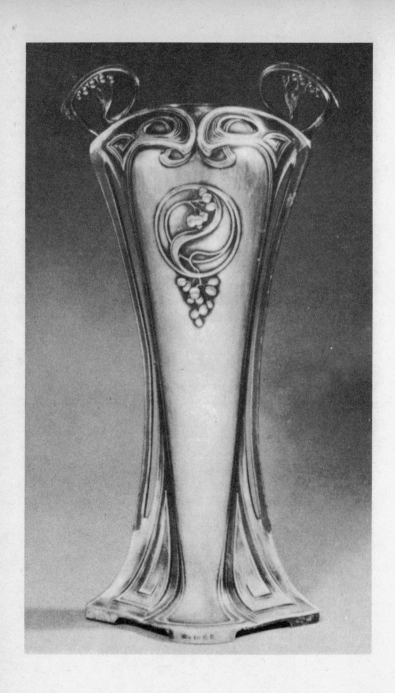

Introduction

By whatever name it was known—and it was known by many names in different countries—the style now commonly referred to as Art Nouveau was not only one of the shortest-lived art movements of modern times, it also was one of the most elusive. Even today it still defies a lucid and encompassing definition, partly because it extended beyond the realm of the graphic, partly because, during its brief span of life, the style underwent a metamorphosis, and partly because its interpretation varied from country to country and often from artist to artist and from artisan to artisan.

Yet Art Nouveau possessed in its heyday a fascination for those surfeited by art forms that either slavishly copied the forms of earlier periods or created innovations within the broad outlines of those earlier forms and by artists and artisans who did little more than refine or redefine the traditional.

Within recent years there has been a rediscovery of Art Nouveau. At the moment its various manifestations are surging back into popularity. It is being reexamined, reappraised, and—from the standpoint of art as investment—it is being reevaluated. The reasons for this curious retrospective scrutiny are almost as elusive as the style itself, but perhaps they have at least some of their roots in protest—that disturbing, depressing, yet stimulating mood in which such a large part of the world has been caught up during the past few years.

Although Art Nouveau was shaped in part by specific art movements that had preceded it and prototypes of it may be found in the work of earlier artists, it almost literally burst into being in England and in various countries or regions of Europe in the 1890's. But by 1905 it had largely run its creative course, although commercial adaptations of the style continued through the First World War.

Proof of the current interest in the movement is to be found in the prices presently being paid for creations in this style that range from posters to metalwork and include such specifics as: glass and pottery by Émile Gallé, one of the foremost practitioners of Art Nouveau in France; glass and jewelry objects by René Lalique; glass by the American Louis Comfort Tiffany; furniture designed by Scotland's Charles Rennie Mackintosh; and certain late-nineteenth- and early-twentieth-century productions of the Rookwood Pottery and other "art" potteries of this period.

Not long ago an Art Nouveau armchair by Mackintosh sold at auction in London for more than $1,000. Early and rare vases and bowls by Gallé have brought close to $1,000. Art Nouveau lithographs have sold in recent months for several hundred dollars each. Tiffany glass from the James Coats/Brian Connelly collection brought what appeared to many observers to be almost astronomical prices ($2,750 for a red glass vase) at a Parke-Bernet Galleries auction in New York City in late 1966, and prices of lesser Tiffany creations are continuing to soar as the supply dwindles. It is not uncommon to see Rookwood vases selling for $100 and more or Weller and Roseville pottery productions influenced by the style bringing $50, $75, and more. Van Briggle pottery made in Denver, Colorado, earlier in this century is beginning to attract collector attention with the likelihood that prices will soon ascend.

Relatively neglected thus far, however, have been the thousands of commercial productions reflecting the influence of Art Nouveau that were turned out in this country and elsewhere from the early twentieth century until about 1925 or 1930 in forms ranging from manicure sets to trinket boxes and from napkin rings to toast racks. These are of far less intrinsic merit or extrinsic value than those individual productions that emerged when the style was in full bloom. Despite this, as well as the fact that they are derided by meditative critics and devotees of the art in its purest form, hundreds of these commercial objects may have an appeal to collectors with modest pocketbooks.

Art Nouveau influences may be found in literally thousands of early twentieth-century objects that are still slumbering in dresser drawers or attic corners, as well as in others that are now beginning to gravitate toward the antiques shops. These include items of jewelry, souvenir spoons, watch fobs, condiment sets, ink stands, puff jars, hair receivers, pocket knives, letter openers, cigar containers, hat-pins, shaving brushes, barrettes, toothbrush bottles, court plaster cases, stamp boxes, pipes—these and scores of other items once in everyday use.

It is with these commercial, readily accessible, and fairly inexpensive objects that this book will primarily, but not exclusively, concern itself. In order to bring the Art Nouveau movement into sharper focus, we also will discuss, though briefly, some of the creations that emerged from the gifted imaginations and talented hands of Tiffany, Gallé, Lalique, and such stalwarts of the movement as Aubrey Beardsley, Henri van de Velde, and Victor Horta to which the more affluent and perhaps more discriminating collectors may address themselves.

Numerous collectible objects will be described in the pages that follow which, although not strictly Art Nouveau, reflect certain influences of the movement and which, although not of enormous value or potential, are intriguing or interesting and deserve to be preserved, if for little other reason than that they reflect the taste and the handiwork of our ancestors.

Many of the more striking examples of Art Nouveau are now preserved in museums or housed in private collections. An exhibition paying tribute to the American architect Louis Sullivan, who worked in the Art Nouveau style, was held in Chicago as early as 1956. In 1957 the Museum of Modern Art in New York City held an exhibition featuring work by Antonio Gaudí y Cornet, who had created striking architectural conceptions in Barcelona. Another exhibition at the Museum of Modern Art in 1959 focused on Art Nouveau design at the turn of this century. A Louis Comfort Tiffany exhibition in New York City in 1958 served to stimulate renewed interest in the achievements of this extraordinary craftsman and innovator. The Pasadena Art Museum staged an exhibit in 1965 of posters in the *Jugendstil* (the German version of Art Nouveau) style. And the Museum of Modern Art in New York City held a "Hector Guimard" exhibition in the spring of 1970, which included works in furniture, wallpaper, graphics, architectural design, and Paris metro designs and photographs by this multifaceted artist. This exhibit moved on from New York to San Francisco, Toronto, and Paris.

But prior to the resurgence of American interest in this period, exhibitions had been held in Europe, and as far back as 1936 Professor Nikolaus Pevsner had heralded Art Nouveau as an independent style in a brilliant study, *Pioneers of Modern Design from William Morris to Walter Gropius.* Other detailed studies have subsequently appeared. However, none of these, to my knowledge, has done more than mention and then dismiss the commercial productions of the first three decades of this century.

Quite recently several new editions of the work of Aubrey Beardsley have appeared, indicating an awakening of interest in the style as expressed in the graphic arts.

Certainly the Art Nouveau bandwagon has started rolling, and it may reach high gear in the near future. Those who view collectible objects that are not yet legitimate antiques

as an investment—and their numbers are becoming legion—
may, therefore, wish to keep an eye out for creations in this
style that may still be plucked from the shops or private
holders at "reasonable" prices—reasonable at least by comparison with what they may be a few years from now.

The diminishing supply and increasing prices of antiques
from the eighteenth century and earlier are exerting pressure
on even affluent collectors to cast about for the collectible
objects of later periods. Sales held by such major auction
establishments as Parke-Bernet, Sotheby's, and Christie's in
1966 and 1967 devoted entirely to Art Nouveau have already
generated mounting interest in the creations in this style
and have started some prices spiraling. But it is likely that the
spiral has only just begun.

By and large—and alas! and alack!—collectors tend to become addicted to fad and fashion. They seek what's in style,
pushing prices up. Art Nouveau already may be well on its
way to becoming the next primary collector fashion. In such
an event, look for prices to soar.

I

Identifying Art Nouveau

THIS SILVER BONBON TRAY OF 1906 UNDOUBTEDLY IMPARTED FLAVOR TO THE TIDBITS SERVED FROM IT. *Unger Brothers.*

ALTHOUGH ART NOUVEAU is the name commonly accepted today in the United States, England, and France for the new style that began flowering in several countries in the 1890's, it was known by other names in other countries: *Jugendstil* in Germany; *Sezessionsstil* in Austria; *Modernismo* in Spain; *Stile floreale* and also *Stile liberty* in Italy; *Paling stijl* and also *Le Style des Vingt* in Belgium.

The new style followed hard on the heels of the style called *historicism,* against which it was an urgent revolt but in which, nevertheless, it had its beginnings. And despite the fact that its proponents and practitioners heralded it as indeed a new style, Robert Schmutzler in his commendable and thorough study of the movement, *Art Nouveau,* offers convincing evidence that its roots went back well into the eighteenth century.

We will not be concerned here with the various influences on the style; these have been delineated in several serious studies in addition to Mr. Schmutzler's, and the reader who wants to investigate the background of the movement in detail will find a list of helpful works in the Selected Bibliography.

The name Art Nouveau itself derived from a shop, *Maison de l'Art Nouveau,* operated at 22 rue de Provence, Paris, by Samuel Bing, a native of Hamburg, Germany, and originally an importer of handcrafts and other arts from Japan. Bing decided to create a market for the work of artists and artisans who had turned to new modes of expression.* In December, 1895, he held his first *Salon de l'Art Nouveau,* which focused widespread attention on stained glass executed by Louis Comfort Tiffany from designs created by Henri de Toulouse-Lautrec, Pierre Bonnard, Eugène Grasset, and others, as well as on Tiffany's own glass creations and those by Émile Gallé: on graphic art by Aubrey Beardsley, the American William H. Bradley, and others; and on jewelry by René Lalique, together with other representations in the new style.

Art Nouveau, invading the decorative and applied arts, found its firmest expression in ornamental elements. Even furniture assumed an aura of the ornamental. Among the characteristics most frequently associated with the style is the whiplash line—an undulating coil, sometimes attenuated, sometimes dilated—that often in the delineation of the human form, particularly in the later commercial productions, found expression in the long, flowing locks of sylphlike women.

Asymmetry was another predominant characteristic, often finding its expression in the arrangement of the ornamental elements. Nature itself provided inspiration for many artists and artisans of the new style, and one often encounters in Art Nouveau designs deep-sea creatures, the butterfly, the peacock, floral elements (particularly stems), seaweed, and so on. These representations were stylized—contorted, imbued with sinuosity, impregnated with mystery, melancholy, or languor. Stylized flowers were of special fascination. From stalks artists created with their languid curves; if blossoms were depicted, they were usually pale rather than bright. In numerous graphic creations one encounters the sunflower and the lily with their aesthetic associations and the peacock and the swan with their consanguinity with narcissism.

When human figures are incorporated in the design, it is the female who predominates, almost invariably imbued in the

* Bing, a prime mover in calling attention to Art Nouveau, in 1896 presented an exhibition of paintings by Edvard Munch, of Norway, some of whose work was in the *Jugendstil* tradition.

earlier phases of the art with solemnity or melancholy, and in the later commercial phases with either insipidity or sexuality. Relative to this concern with the female, Peter Selz comments in *Art Nouveau: Art and Design at the Turn of the Century:* "The interest in the bud and the young girl suggests that the ideal world of the Art Nouveau artist was far removed from what is usually thought of as the 'Gay Nineties.' He [the artist] seemed to prefer a melancholy, nostalgic expression to unbridled gaiety or joy. Everything remains in a state of unfulfillment; there is perhaps eager expectation, but it never seems to go beyond the threshhold."

And, as Alan M. Fern comments in the same book, artists of the new style "tried to evoke a peculiar sense of movement and mood." Not infrequently, and particularly in the case of Aubrey Beardsley, the mood evoked was foreboding, sometimes evil. More frequently, it was a mood of melancholy or nostalgia. Often, too, there was an evocation of the mysterious —a sort of graphic cryptograph, the meaning of which begged for intense scrutiny.

Along with the whiplash line, there was a quality of linearity in much of the work in the Art Nouveau manner. Many full-length figures appear to be extraordinarily tall and wraith-like. Bodies lean as if swayed by a continuing gust of wind. Some appear as apparitions and seem to float. Linearity also characterizes such Art Nouveau creations as furniture, glass, and jewelry, and pervades the surface of much of the period's architecture. The total effect is one of lightness, never of massiveness, even in the entrances for the Paris métro created by the French architect Hector Guimard at the turn of this century or in the almost fantastic ironwork railings and metal entrances designed by Antonio Gaudí in Barcelona.

A sense of movement is conveyed by varied devices in Art Nouveau productions: clouds that appear to move gently, water that always ripples, forms that writhe, swift breezes, flowers and other vegetation that sway languidly, flames that taper to a point.

Much Art Nouveau is basically ethereal. There are dim and shadowy effects, an aura of impermanence and mystery, living creatures that bear kinship with both man and animal and yet are neither, fragility everywhere, and often senuousness. Some creations of the new art appear to have been designed with the specific intention of generating a sense of nostalgia, of loneliness, of sympathy with those who are not quite like ourselves. The close affinity of Art Nouveau with the art of Japan has been stressed by many writers in this field, and the influence of Japanese artists upon those of the Art Nouveau period can scarcely be overestimated. Debts were owed, too, to William Blake and William Morris. Art Nouveau is suggestive and evocative; it can lead to daydreams that embroider the shadowy images presented or weave the plot of a story that has been barely hinted at.

These characteristics that we have mentioned are primarily feminine in nature. Decadence, too, has been called a key to the style, but Robert Schmutzler perhaps sums it up best when he says, "The Aesthete and his brother, the Dandy, are the true key figures of Art Nouveau." [1]

But Art Nouveau was indeed a new art, even though ties with the past were never completely severed. Its battle was with historicism, which imitated and adapted numerous styles of the past. The curve replaced the angle and the straight line, although in the late phase of Art Nouveau there was some inclination toward the rectilinear. The protest against historicism was both collective and individual, and it extended to all that was commonplace, mediocre, or bourgeois. Still, it shared its characteristic feature of asymmetry with the rococo and borrowed, at least in France, from Gothic.

The style has been called two-dimensional; yet it also was three-dimensional, especially in Belgium. And here it must be emphasized that although Art Nouveau emerged almost simultaneously in several geographical areas, it possessed its own nationalistic individualism with conceptual variations from England to France, from France to Germany, from Ger-

THIS MAGNIFICENT TIFFANY GLASS WINDOW IS AN OUTSTANDING EX-
AMPLE OF THE ART NOUVEAU STYLE. *Lightner Museum, St. Augustine,
Florida.*

many to Barcelona. If the style flourished in its two-dimensional form in the graphic arts, it flourished also for awhile in its three-dimensional form in furniture, glass, metal work, and pottery.

Stephan Tschudi Madsen says it is possible to distinguish four different primary aspects of Art Nouveau: (1) an abstract plastic conception of form (Belgium art being an outstanding example); (2) a linear and symbolic aspect (particularly in Scotland); (3) a floral aspect, inspired by plants (notable in France); and (4) a constructive and geometrical aspect (evident in Austria and Germany).[2]

Actually, too, Art Nouveau had interests in common with the widely publicized Arts and Crafts movement, whose prime mover was the versatile William Morris in England. This movement sought to bring about a unification of all the arts and crafts and to reform them as a rebellion against the widespread mediocrity engendered by the machine and its mass production methods. So, too, Art Nouveau sought a synthesis of the arts, but, as Peter Selz put it, "One of the essential aspects of Art Nouveau was the acceptance of technology and the machine as a means toward creating a new style, without however, elevating functionalism to an esthetic principle."[3]

Regardless of its faults, its limitations, and its ultimate failure, Art Nouveau at least freed art from its conventions and broke sharply with tradition. Its new expression helped pave the way for the artistic rebellions that have followed up to the present day.

What are some of the names most frequently associated with the new style in addition to those already mentioned? In Brussels there was Victor Horta, whose Tassel house, built in 1893, has been termed the first of the fully-blown Art Nouveau buildings. Subsequently he designed the Maison du Peuple for the Socialist Party in Belgium and built other houses, the decoration and furnishing of which he also supervised.

Another Belgian, Henri van de Velde, extended the influence of Art Nouveau to painting, architecture, and design.

An example of commercial Art Nouveau in the picture frame field. This one is of silver by Unger Brothers, which, interestingly, supplied all frames with pictures. Frame shown here was etched and pierced. *Unger Brothers.*

And through his writing, he helped interpret and popularize the new style.

The prime figure in Great Britain was Charles Rennie Mackintosh, the Glasgow architect and artist who also designed furniture and accessories and with whom are customarily associated the names of his wife, the former Margaret Macdonald, and her sister, Frances, both artists. Mackintosh designed the Glasgow School of Art, in which the geometric phase of Art Nouveau was evident.

In England, in addition to Aubrey Beardsley, there were Arthur Mackmurdo, who had established in 1884 *The Century Guild Hobby Horse,* a periodical that was the precursor of strictly Art Nouveau periodicals, and who, in addition to his work in the graphic arts designed rather rectangular furniture; Charles Ricketts, who founded the *Dial,* did extraordinary book binding, and illustrated works by Oscar Wilde; Charles Annesley Voysey, architect; and Albert Gilbert, sculptor in metals.

The German version of Art Nouveau, the *Jugendstil,* emerged with the founding of the periodical *Pan* in 1895, although it actually took its name from the magazine *Jugend,* established in Munich a year later. Among the leaders associated with the new art in Germany were August Endell, who designed the Elvira Studio in Munich in 1897; Otto Eckmann, whose specialty was floral art; Peter Behrens, painter, designer, and architect of the Munich school; Hermann Obrist, sculptor and potter; and Bernhard Pankok, who worked in the fields of sculpture, the applied arts, and architecture.

The two prime centers of the art in France were Nancy— where Émile Gallé worked as an artisan in glass, ceramics, and furniture design and Louis Majorelle produced furniture in the new style—and Paris—whose best-known leader in the movement was Hector Guimard, the architect, although René Lalique's jewelry and glass creations are perhaps better known in America. In France, too, Henri de Toulouse-Lautrec created his world-famous posters in the Art Nouveau style.

Aubrey Beardsley's design for **Morte d'Arthur,** shown here in the negative, was published in the october, 1894, issue of "The Studio."

Joseph Hoffmann and Joseph Olbrich were distinguished exponents of the art in Austria, where it flowered later than in other countries and where its use of geometrical figures in decoration differentiated it from what flourished elsewhere. Gustav Klimt, painter and decorator, Kolomon Moser, designer, and the Vienna architect Otto Wagner also adopted this style.

In Holland, there was Jan Toorop, the painter, whose special kind of Art Nouveau was reflected primarily in the ornaments he created. Edvard Munch, also a painter, is the one name most frequently associated with this art in Norway. And in the United States, there were the names already mentioned: Louis Comfort Tiffany, the great glass innovator; Louis Sullivan, outstanding Chicago architect, who designed, among other buildings, the Rothschild Department Store and the Chicago Auditorium; and William H. Bradley, whose art work in Chicago resembled Beardsley's.

Posters, book binding and decoration, glass, pottery, furniture, architecture, jewelry, textiles, metal work: these are the fields in which Art Nouveau found its most effective expression during its short life, although in its subsequent commercial phase its influence extended to numerous other areas. As Nikolaus Pevsner wrote, although Art Nouveau extended to architecture, it was primarily a matter of decoration, largely of the surface.

The colors that predominated in the new style were pale grays, greens, reds, blues, violet, mauve, and pink, together with a chalky white. Bright colors were almost invariably eschewed for pastels.

With the Paris International Exposition of 1900 the movement had reached its climax; by 1903, its ebb had ceased.

II

Art Nouveau Glass

Favrile glass vase by Louis C. Tiffany standing 16⅛ inches high was manufactured by Tiffany Studios. *Collection, The Museum of Modern Art, New York City, Phyllis B. Lambert Fund.*

CURRENTLY, the preeminent position among American producers of glasswares, rather loosely and broadly lumped together under the category of "art glass," is occupied by Louis Comfort Tiffany. This statement may be debated by the admirers of Frederick Carder, Victor Durand, and a handful of other artisans and designers who also turned out some magnificent creations in glass earlier in this century; but the fact remains that the Tiffany name is more widely known among collectors in general, and his productions command the greatest respect among both nascent and experienced collectors.

Outstanding Tiffany pieces have risen sharply in value in recent years; prices have actually doubled in the past twenty years. Although the climb in values had been under way for about a decade, prices commanded at a sale of a collection of choice pieces assembled by James Coats and the late Brian Connelly in October, 1966, were almost shockingly high. The auction, held at the Parke-Bernet Galleries, was widely publicized beforehand, although the collection consisted of ony 76 pieces—75 vases and one bowl. The collection brought a total of $84,450.

An ochre and blue vase of Favrile glass, inscribed "L. C. Tiffany" and once in Mr. Tiffany's personal collection, brought $3,250. Three other vases brought $3,000, $2,800, and $2,750, respectively.

Tiffany lamps in Art Nouveau designs have also been bringing increasingly high prices in the past few years. A price of $2,300 was paid for one decorated with peacock feathers at a Parke-Bernet sale in March, 1967.

The majority of Tiffany glass productions after 1890 were strictly Art Nouveau. It is likely that the present sharp demand for them is due partly to the revival of interest in Art Nouveau and partly to a recently awakening awareness of Tiffany's artistic genius.

Several excellent books have been devoted in the past few years either wholly or in part to Tiffany and his work, and these are listed in the Selected Bibliography for those who wish to study the man and his productions in depth. The sketch that follows, therefore, will be brief.

Louis Comfort Tiffany was born in 1848. His father, Charles L. Tiffany, founded the famous Tiffany & Company of New York City. It is surprising how many people think that Louis Tiffany was a member of the firm of Tiffany & Company and that the jewelry and metal accessories sold by this company were his creations.

The younger Tiffany, however, did not follow in his father's footsteps, except for a brief period (and he did create a limited amount of jewelry). Instead he turned first to painting and shortly afterward to the applied arts. By 1880, Tiffany was well on his way to becoming this country's best-known interior decorator. His renown was reflected in the selection of Associated Artists (in which Candace Wheeler and Samuel Coleman were associated with Tiffany) to re-decorate the White House.

Tiffany soon turned also to producing stained glass windows and mosaics and the Tiffany Glass Company was incorporated in 1885. It was subsequently reorganized and became known as the Tiffany Glass and Decorating Company. During the closing decade of last century, stained glass windows were in high fashion for palatial residences, public buildings, and even more modest homes, and the new company produced them in some abundance after designs by Tiffany himself. The Vanderbilts and the Whitelaw Reids were among his clients. Tiffany also began producing mosaics of iridescent glass in combination with inlays of mother-of-pearl and semiprecious stones.

Tiffany's relationship with Samuel Bing, who gave him great encouragement, and his "discovery" of Émile Gallé's Art Nouveau glass at the Paris Exposition of 1889 provided him with new inspirational directions and turned him toward the Art Nouveau style, in which he saw the possibilities of a new expression for his talents.

Tiffany exhibited a chapel featuring beautiful glass windows at the Chicago World's Fair, where the work attracted major attention. Meanwhile, he was perfecting a new type of glass he was to call Favrile (a modification of the old English word *fabrile,* meaning handmade) that was to cause a commotion in the world of glass production.

Tiffany had produced his first figure window in 1877. These windows depended largely upon transmitted light for their play of colors. Here is how Tiffany himself described his innovations in glass in 1913 in an advertisement-brochure for the ecclesiastical department of Tiffany Studios (which developed as a workshop out of the Tiffany Glass and Decorating Company): "Scientist as well as artist, Mr. Tiffany was averse to using any paints or stains whatever, even for the flesh tints, though vitreous colors were employed and fired and fused into the glass. He rebelled against the restrictions placed upon him by the limitations of the glass then procurable and resolved to find something better. Then began the experiments which were continued persistently for years until he discovered a means of producing with quasi-uniform results a material fraught with colors, surfaces and textures in infinite variety and varying degrees of transparency. It was not only opalescent, deriving its play of color largely by transmitted light, but it was also iridescent with a permanent metallic lustre, emitting rainbow effects by light reflected from the surfaces. The discovery was epoch-making. It marked a transition from commercialism to art, resulting from the scientific experiments of an artist.

"Mr. Tiffany elected to call his discovery Tiffany Favrile glass."

The brochure continues: "Plans for the manufacture of

this glass were perfected, but not with a view to mathematical accuracy as in the average commercial factory. The purpose is rather to seek chance or accidental effects which can not be divorced from fire products, and which so enrich the field of the artist. Though essentially a scientific product, therefore, Tiffany Favrile glass varies sufficiently in the process of making to produce constantly increasing color blendings which give the designer a range that is boundless."

This glass was produced at the Tiffany Furnaces (the name to which the Stourbridge Glass Company in Corona, New York, was changed in 1902—and of which Louis C. Tiffany was president) for the exclusive use at that time of the Tiffany Studios. (The name was changed again in 1920, to Louis C. Tiffany Furnaces, Inc., according to Albert Christian Revi.[1])

The majority of those who have written with authority about Louis Comfort Tiffany in recent years have contended that he held himself in high esteem and rather constantly sought the limelight; this seems unquestionably true, although his high opinion of his own genius was shared by a great many experts. The contention seems further borne out by the following comments in the 1913 brochure from which we have just quoted: "Opalescent, iridescent, imperishable and requiring no paint, Tiffany Favrile glass is the basis of all Tiffany windows. This exclusive basic material surpasses the best of the Mediaeval glass workers, whose art reached its zenith in the thirteenth century."

The brochure further claims that general recognition had been given the Tiffany Studios "as the greatest exponent of progressive American art," adding: "It [the sincerity of Tiffany's work] may also account for the giving of credit to Mr. Louis C. Tiffany personally for a valuable form of neo-Classicism resulting from a fusion of the best modern spirit with an assimilated spirit of the best Mediaeval creations in colored glass."

Tiffany's Favrile glass was produced in numerous objects

for household use and decoration, ranging from a multitude of vases to tablewares. Mr. Revi gives a large share of the credit for the success of Tiffany glass to Arthur J. Nash—who came to America from England, was a principal in establishing the Stourbridge Glass Company in Corona, and was subsequently a ranking official and stockholder of Tiffany Furnaces and later of the Louis C. Tiffany Furnaces, Inc.—and to his sons, A. Douglas Nash and Leslie H. Nash.

With their pearl-like sheen, Tiffany's lustered glasswares bore close resemblance to the surface of centuries-old glass long buried in the humid earth. Numerous lustered effects were obtained by the use of various colors and densities of glass—colors that ranged from blues to gold, from green to black, from red to milky white.

Tiffany was an indefatigable worker, and his continuing experiments resulted in the creation of new glass designs and forms—some evolving from shapes of ancient glass, a number of fine examples of which he had in his personal collection.

His lamps and lighting devices were put to work in his interior decorating ventures, and near the close of the last century his company produced lamps from his own designs for public sale. His leaded glass shades, far superior to the majority of somewhat similar shades popular early in the twentieth century, were manufactured in variety, and the demand for these is at a peak right now. His large chandeliers are fetching record prices, even though inferior imitations of them are available for lower sums.

Typical of the Art Nouveau style is Tiffany's lamp with a design patterned after a cluster of lilies and with Morning Glory lustered shades and a bronze base. Variations were made in different sizes and with varying numbers of shades.

Also taking its motif from nature was his Wisteria lamp. And there were others with motifs of dragonflies, daffodils, roses, pansies, magnolia blossoms, poppies, geraniums, and other flowers, and with motifs representing such creatures as snails (and shells), scarabs, butterflies, and so on.

Pure Art Nouveau was his Nautilus lamp with its shade in the shape of a spiral chambered shell of opal leaded glass and its bronze base in the shape of a mermaid with long, flowing hair and arms extended upward to grasp the shade. A fine example of the Nautilus in the collection of Mr. Revi is illustrated in his *American Art Nouveau Glass.*

Many of the lamps were actually designed by talented Tiffany employees. Hundreds of Favrile glass lamps and shades were turned out under various trade names and in varied shapes and designs. A choice one was a miniature five-piece "night lamp," standing about 13½ inches tall, with gold-lustered glass base and shade, an opal glass shaft with green leaves, a small gold-lustered glass chimney, and metal collar and socket. The Favrile glass pieces of this lamp are signed "L. C. T."

The multitudinous vases made by Tiffany in flower forms with designs of petals and leaves in various colors, including greens, reds, pink, yellows, white, blues, and purple were high Art Nouveau. Highly desired by collectors are Tiffany vases and other objects that are internally lustered and are frequently referred to by collectors and dealers as "paper-weight" type (a phrase frowned upon by Mr. Revi). Most frequently the decorative motifs for these derive from flowers and occasionally from sea life. These layered pieces command high prices and are eagerly sought.

Tiffany vases were also turned out in gourd shapes, bulbous shapes, and free forms. Glass objects made by Tiffany embraced such types as agate or laminated glass, produced from a melt of different colored opaque glasses worked together; Cypriote imitating the textures of ancient buried glass; Lava, mimicking volcanic molten rock; cameo, produced from two or more layers of glass with the designs etched by acid; and intaglio, with designs cut into the outer layer.

Tiffany also made reactive glass, with color changes obtained by reheating; flashed glass, widely called "pastel Tiffany"; and millefiori types, utilizing vari-colored rods of

TABLE LAMP OF GLASS WITH SHAFT
AND BASE IN FORM OF A TREE TRUNK
OF BRASS. *Lightner Museum, St.
Augustine, Florida.*

TIFFANY HANGING SHADE WITH
GLASS OF YELLOW TO WHITE COLORS,
SET IN BRONZE. *Lightner Museum,
St. Augustine, Florida.*

TIFFANY VASE, CA. 1900–1910, FREE-BLOWN, OF LIGHT
BLUE GLASS WITH IRIDESCENCE; 2½ INCHES HIGH. *The
Corning Museum of Glass, Corning Glass Center,
Corning, New York.*

glass, among others. The processes for producing these varieties of glass are admirably described in Mr. Revi's *American
Art Nouveau Glass,* which is highly recommended to the
reader who wants further knowledge of processes and patents.

Marks on Tiffany glass include the initials "L.C.T.," "L. C.
Tiffany/Favrile," and, on outstanding pieces, "Louis C.
Tiffany/Favrile"—frequently in combination with numbers
and letters, all incised in the glass, and paper labels with
company trademarks.

In addition to lamps, shades, and vases, Tiffany Art Nouveau glass, often in combination with metal, was made in
the form of bowls, plates, pitchers, stemwares of numerous
kinds, tazzas, mugs, costume decorative accessories, tumblers,
tiles, plaques, mirrors, inkstands, cigarette boxes, tobacco
jars, finger bowls, and other decorative and household objects.
Most of those that fall into the decorative category were produced by Tiffany Studios after the turn of the century and up
until about the time the studios closed.

Tiffany wares were not cheap when originally offered, and
they were sold through exclusive outlets, Tiffany & Company
in New York City being one example. Favrile glass flower
vases were available in 1915 at prices of $5 to $500—an extensive range indeed and high at the top! Jardinieres with
wire mesh cost as much as $50. Carved glass crystal pieces
were as high as $200, and the larger shapes in cameo and rock
crystal brought $120 to $175. Library and table lamps were
especially perilously priced, ranging from $40 to $350 without shades. A lily stems lamp with daffodil shade commanded
$155.

It should be emphasized that not all Tiffany glass objects
were strictly Art Nouveau in character; a good many imitated
classic forms. But scores of objects derived their inspiration
from nature, and Tiffany himself certainly was the chief
American exponent of the new style. He apparently delighted
in devising new and unconventional forms, often exotic and
senuous in appeal.

Tiffany vases, by and large, provide outstanding examples of Art Nouveau style, and this is particularly true of those whose spiraling lines seem to be in motion and whose forms appear to stretch upward from their bases. The convolution of his leaf designs suggests the whiplash line so typical of much Art Nouveau. Movement, too, is constantly suggested by his iridescent surfaces which shimmer and change tone under varying degrees of light and by patterns that seem to flow and ebb with an almost mystical asymmetry.

Although Tiffany designed new forms, these are rarely complicated and are often characterized by continuous and frequently sinuous contours that impart an exotic flavor, yet certainly do not shock contemporary taste.

Tiffany's decorative motifs after 1890 were shared by many other artists and artisans who turned to the new style: leaves, tendrils, and blossoms of vines and flowers; seaweed and other marine elements, including anemone, fish, and echinoderm, as well as pond lilies; the peacock feather, which Tiffany utilized in a variety of ways with emphasis on the "peacock eye"; multicolored streaks, especially in laminated and heat-sensitive glass; waves; and insects. Among Tiffany's favorite flowers were lilies, poppies, tulips, gladiola, daisies, and morning glories. Blossoms, as well as leaves and stems, were often stylized to convey a sense of motion and a continuity of convolvular line.

He adapted these elements of nature with remarkable ingenuity to suggest the masses and whirling lines so typical of Art Nouveau, and for their coloration he devised an extraordinarily extensive range of hues and shades. The sense of motion communicated by his whirling masses was also suggestive of growth—the evolution of form and being with which numerous artists of the new style were preoccupied.

Not long after this country entered World War I, Tiffany relinquished his role in the Tiffany Furnaces and the works were bought by A. Douglas Nash, who operated them as the A. Douglas Nash Corporation for several years, failing at about the time of the depression of 1931. Tiffany Studios continued its operations until 1928, although its stock had been offered for sale in 1920. Tiffany himself died at the age of 85 in January, 1933.

As Louis Comfort Tiffany was the greatest American exponent of Art Nouveau, so Émile Gallé was certainly its foremost practitioner in glass in France. Unlike Tiffany, Gallé did follow in the footsteps of his father, who operated a glass and pottery workshop and also made furniture. But, like Tiffany, he studied art early in his career.

At the age of 27, Émile Gallé opened a glassworks in partnership with his father, subsequently establishing his own factory in Nancy, which became a major center of the Art Nouveau movement in Europe.

Gallé was an ardent and conscientious student of nature, devoting hours to journeying through the countryside, filling notebook after notebook with the sketches that provided a basis for many of his glass and pottery designs. And it is in fact designs taken direct from nature that provide the motifs for the decoration of most Gallé glass. Also, and common to other exponents of the Art Nouveau style, Gallé was influenced profoundly by Oriental art, and particularly by Japanese glass techniques and colors.

Early in his career, this great French artisan concentrated on enameled glass, later turning to cameo techniques, of which he achieved remarkable mastery. The bulk of Gallé's glass productions are decorative pieces; only a comparatively few utilitarian items, including powder boxes, were produced. Sometimes he combined enameling and cameo techniques on the same piece.

Both his enameled glass and his cameo creations reflect Gallé's intense knowledge of and preoccupation with organic forms: his surfaces are alive with flowers, vines, stalks, leaves, insects, vegetables, bodies of water—all executed with an inventive artistry that has seldom been surpassed in glass. For him, the forms of nature were paramount, and under his

GLASS ART NOUVEAU VASE CREATED BY EMILE GALLÉ OF NANCY, FRANCE. *Lightner Museum, St. Augustine, Florida.*

MAGNIFICENT CAMEO VASE BY EMILE GALLÉ, WHOSE SIGNATURE MAY BE SEEN AT LEFT NEAR THE BOTTOM. *Courtesy, Victoria and Albert Museum, London.*

CARVED TRANSLUCENT PINK AND BLUE GLASS VASE MADE BY EMILE GALLÉ, ABOUT 1900. *Collection, The Museum of Modern Art, New York City, purchase.*

ministrations they assumed a beauty that not only brought admiration in his lifetime but that still arouse it today, even among urban dwellers, removed from a proximity to nature in its myriad manifestations.

The majority of utilitarian pieces are found in enameled glass with a basic color that approaches a blue-gray, sometimes smoky with an amber tint. Green and clear enameled pieces were also produced, but later in Gallé's career, according to William Ernest Mouser, Jr., and Peggy Joyce Gurn.[2] In enameled glass one finds bowls, decanter sets, some table pieces such as cups and saucers and cream and sugar sets, and, of course, vases that were produced in far greater numbers than any other individual objects.

The enameled decorations, executed with painstaking skill, featured pastel colors of brown, blue, green, and gray, and the work itself reminds one of the delicate, sometimes almost haunting tracery made by snow crystals upon a window. Pastels were also utilized for some of the cameo glass, but the bulk of the cameo pieces show stronger colors—green, brown, yellow, purple, blue, red, and black. The last two are the rarest of the Gallé colors.[3]

Although at the outset of his work with the cameo technique Gallé made a number of relatively small pieces, his creations became progressively larger, for a while, the largest finding their way to various expositions, for which purpose some undoubtedly were specifically intended.

The earliest cameo pieces, and consequently the scarcest, employed a single color, but several colors were utilized later, requiring meticulous workmanship to complete the designs. By varying the thicknesses of various layers of the colored glass, the artist achieved the illusion of more colored layers than were actually involved. Typically Art Nouveau are the flowing curves of stems and tendrils and tree trunks and limbs, the asymmetry of leaves, pods, and buds, the use of cobweblike tracery, and the incorporation into design of insects. But whereas many other Art Nouveau practitioners concentrated on rippling and sometimes turbulently active water, Gallé's lake scenes were most frequently placid. Birds, however, are pictured in flight to further the illusion of movement.

The shapes of Gallé's glass objects show less inventiveness than Tiffany's: most are relatively traditional—bulbous, ovoid, squatty, or bulbous bases with long, slender necks— or amphora types reminiscent of Greek art, or asymmetrical. But the manner in which Gallé merged his ornament with form is extraordinary.

Little has been written about the work of Émile Gallé, but an excellent short introduction was presented by Mr. Mouser and Mrs. Gurn in an article in the July, 1968, issue of *The Antiques Journal,* in which the authors emphasized that virtually all of his work bears his signature, sometimes on the bottom of a piece but at other times incorporated into a part of the design so that it is difficult to locate. The authors report that the only pieces not signed were component parts of a set, of which a single piece was signed. The artist died in 1904, and pieces produced after his death bear a star before his name.

Gallé's work met with such success that he was ultimately forced to abandon the production of strictly individual pieces and turn to mass production methods, which included the use of the same molds for similar shapes with varying surface treatments. Some objects were blown into molds that incorporated designs. Acid etching was used both to produce some textured surfaces and to produce a satiny finish. And some pieces were free blown.

Gallé made some particularly fascinating lamps in cameo glass. Outstanding among them was one with a cameo shade featuring cutting on both interior and exterior surfaces and with a cast bronze base of the Three Graces, clad in long, flowing robes, whose upstretched arms hold the shade. This lamp is in the collection of Mrs. Gurn, of Amarillo, Texas.

Large quantities of Gallé Art Nouveau glass have found their way into private and public collections, so there is a scarcity of pieces available made before his death. Gallé maintained a showroom in London, and advertisements of his glass appeared in periodicals early in this century. One in 1904 commented that his work had been purchased by the Luxembourg, Arts Décoratifs, Kensington, Victoria and Albert, Berlin, Hamburg, and St. Petersburg museums. Many additional museums, of course, now contain examples. A number of Gallé pieces are engraved with quotations, which also are incorporated as a part of the total design.

After mass production methods took over, the Gallé workmen utilized acid etching instead of hand-cutting on wheels for the cameo work, with the inevitable result that quality fell off. Gallé's workshop continued to produce art glass until 1913, however, and the total number of pieces turned out was so large that interesting examples are still available at prices that may seem bargains a decade or two hence.

Rapidly gaining in esteem is the Art Nouveau glass work of René Lalique, better known up till now as a jeweler than as an artisan in glass. Lalique, born in 1865 in a small French village but educated in Paris, began his career as a jewelry designer and achieved distinction in the field even while apprenticed to a firm of jewelry-makers. His fame grew as he subsequently worked for other establishments in Paris before setting himself up as an independent designer, and his creations in jewelry will be discussed in greater detail in Chapter V.

It was his work with stones, especially rock crystal, however, that led Lalique into experimentation with glass—a field in which he achieved phenomenal success. He established a workshop in combination with a sales display building in Paris, and his first major success in this new field came when he was commissioned by the noted perfumer Coty to design scent bottles. The result was well worthy of their world-famous contents.

In 1920, at the age of 60, he founded René Lalique et

VASE OF GREENISH-WHITE
GLASS BY LALIQUE. *Courtesy,
Musée des Arts Décoratifs,
Paris.*

THIS CREATION IN GLASS IN THE ART
NOUVEAU STYLE IS BY RENÉ LALIQUE
AND IS IN THE *Musée des Arts Décoratifs, Paris, by whose courtesy it
is reproduced.*

BOX WITH OPAQUE GLASS BLACK
COVER BY RENÉ LALIQUE. *The Met-
ropolitan Museum of Art, Edward
C. Moore, Jr., gift, 1923.*

Cie at Wingen in the rich French province of Alsace-Lorraine, so long the center of a bitter struggle between France and Germany. The company's production was substantial and varied, ranging from bottles to stemwares, from jewelry boxes to fruit dishes, from lighting fixtures to fascinating figurines.

The majority of Lalique's productions in glass were molded wares, but some combined casting with cutting. Frosted effects were achieved with the use of acids. Decorative effects were sometimes obtained by the application of enamels, sparsely used. In addition to the color imparted by enamels, Lalique also obtained color with the use of colored glass and semitransparent glasses which transmitted diffused light, and rainbow effects were produced by the action of gaseous fumes upon the surface.

Some of Lalique's glass objects were blown, some partly blown, partly molded, and the artist also utilized the cire-perdue (lost wax) technique, in which the original model was made of wax and the final mold was ceramic.

Many collectors today clamor for Lalique's lovely scent bottles, for a series of animals and birds he created in miniature, or for some of the extensive variety of boudoir accessories that range from ungent bottles to charming dresser trays. Far less accessible are his creations in architectural glass that embraced conceptions from entrances to church altars.

By no means was all of Lalique's glass in the Art Nouveau style, but nature provided the motif for much of its adornment: blossoms and vines, curving tendrils, foliage, the peacock and other bird and animal shapes, and nymphs. One encounters, too, the Art Nouveau element of sinuosity in the shapes of many Lalique objects of glass. The collector can identify Lalique pieces by the signature on each.

René Lalique was joined in his work by his son Marc, who has directed the work of the company since his father's death in 1945, with emphasis in recent years upon glass for architecture and interior decoration. In 1965 the company inaugurated a series of annual collector plates of crystal. These are produced in limited editions and at least the first of them was designed by René Lalique's daughter, Marie-Claude Lalique.

Several magazine articles have appeared about the work of Lalique and his son, Marc, including "René Lalique, Artist and Industrialist," by Albert Christian Revi in the April, 1958, issue of *Spinning Wheel;* "Lalique Annual Plates," by Lois B. Herring in the same magazine for November, 1966; and "Lalique's Glass Masterpieces," by Clarence T. Hubbard in the June, 1949, issue of *The Antiques Journal.*

Mr. Hubbard, incidentally, points out that production of Lalique glass ceased from 1939 to 1946 and that the factory itself was demolished, but Marc Lalique subsequently re-established the works, which are still in operation today.

Numerous other artisans in glass worked to produce pieces in the Art Nouveau style between the 1890's and 1910 or later. A large percentage of these, both in the United States and abroad, directed primary attempts toward imitating the work of Tiffany.

Among those working in the new style in the United States were the Nashes, who first worked with and then succeeded Tiffany; the Quezal Art Glass & Decorating Company, established in 1901 in Brooklyn, New York, and spearheaded by a former Tiffany employee, Martin Bach; the Vineland Flint Glass Works, in which Victor Durand was the prime mover, though he was subsequently joined by Martin Bach, Jr., who tried to operate the Quezal factory after his father's death; the Union Glass Company of Somerville, Massachusetts, which produced a glass known as "Kew Blas" in the Art Nouveau style in the 1890's; the Lustre Art Glass Company of Long Island, New York, which produced some late lamp shades with Art Nouveau designs, highly imitative of the Quezal shades; the Steuben Glass Works of Corning, New

York, of which Frederick Carder, an Englishman, was the creative genius, and which produced some wares in Art Nouveau shapes and styles, particularly in a type of glass known as Aurene, closely related to Tiffany's Favrile iridescent glass and much of which was decorated with leaves, vines, and flowers and with trailing threads, as well as in acid-etched cased glass, known as acid cut-back; and the Fostoria Glass Specialty Company of Fostoria, Ohio, which also produced a lustered line of wares with shades in particular decorated with Art Nouveau types of naturalistic leaves and tendrils.

The Imperial Glass Company of Bellaire, Ohio, and the Fenton Art Glass Company of Martins Ferry, Ohio, perhaps better known now among collectors for their Carnival glass, did make "art glass" lines in the Art Nouveau tradition. During the 1920's the former produced iridescent glasswares with decorations of leaves, hearts, and trailing vines, as well as some non-iridescent pieces with decorations consisting of trailing threads of colored glass. These objects were marked with the trade name "Free Hand." Somewhat similar wares were made during the 1920's by Fenton.

A variety of Art Nouveau lamps was made by Handel & Company of Meriden, Connecticut, lines and motifs of the new art being reflected sometimes in the glass shades, sometimes in the metal bases, and sometimes in both. Handel designed metal bases in the shape of leaves and metal standards with sinuous curves resembling flower stalks that supported glass shades in the shape of flowers. Just as Tiffany had done, Handel also created pond lily lamps, some with several branches. The company made other objects, including vases, tazzas, and bowls, decorated with flower, leaf, and vine designs in the flowing Art Nouveau style. Most of the company's products are marked with its name. The beauty of many Handel lamps has begun to be truly appreciated in recent years, and their values have risen considerably.

Several other American glass manufacturers turned out a variety of articles with Art Nouveau-type decor between the

THIS RARE AND BEAUTIFUL
SIGNED QUEZAL LAMP WAS AN
ELEGANT PRODUCTION OF THE
ART NOUVEAU PERIOD. *Mr.
and Mrs. C. C. Pritchard, The
Golden Peacock, St. Augustine, Florida.*

EARLY TWENTIETH-CENTURY QUE-
ZAL VASE BY THE QUEZAL ART
GLASS & DECORATING COMPANY,
BROOKLYN. IRIDESCENT PEARL-
WHITE AND GOLD, PATTERN-MOLDED
AND FREE-BLOWN; 10.25 CENTIME-
TERS TALL. *Corning Museum of
Glass, Corning Glass Center, Corning, New York.*

QUEZAL GLASS SHADE. *Ex-collection of author.*

1890's and about 1915, but many of these were largely inci-
dental to the production of glassware in novel shapes and
designs. Both the Mt. Washington Glass Company of New
Bedford, Massachusetts, and the New England Glass Company (succeeded by the Libbey Glass Company) of Cambridge, Massachusetts, occasionally featured decorations on
some of their novelty art glasses, in styles closely reminiscent
of Art Nouveau. Typical was a Pomona glass pitcher adorned
with a butterfly and sheaves of wheat made by New England
Glass Company, now in the collection of Dr. and Mrs. Walter
Donahue and illustrated in Ray and Lee Grover's *Art Glass
Nouveau*.[4] Some of the Mt. Washington pieces were decorated with sea life and trailing vines and blossoms that were
in spirit closely akin to Art Nouveau, if not precisely in the
mood.

In England, the Art Nouveau spirit permeated some of the
various types of art glass vases and other articles made by the
widely-known firms of Thomas Webb and Sons and Stevens
and Williams, and several other glass houses.

French glass houses, in addition to Gallé's, that turned
out Art Nouveau productions included the Daum brothers
in Nancy, whose glass was usually marked "Daum Nancy";
Eugène Rousseau, who actually anticipated Art Nouveau
style, and his successor, E. B. Léveillé; the Muller brothers
of Luneville, and subsequently of Croismare, whose work
is signed "Muller Frères Luneville" or "Muller, Luneville,"
simply "Muller" or "Luneville," and also with the name
"Muller" or "Croismare," combinations of these words, and
sometimes with the addition of "Nancy"; August J. F. Legras
of Saint-Denis; Cristallerie de Pantin (formerly known by
several other names), whose productions are variously signed
"deVez," "Mont Joy" or "Pantin"; La Verre Français of
Paris; and François Décorchemont, who worked primarily
with the *pâte de verre* technique, a processing used in ancient
times and revived in the nineteenth century.

Some Art Nouveau pieces in cameo glass were made by the

ART NOUVEAU CAMEO BOWL
MARKED "CRISTALLERIE PAN-
TIN" IS CUT FROM PURPLE TO
A CAMPHOR GROUND. *Author's
collection.*

TWO VASES PRODUCED
AT THE STEUBEN GLASS
WORKS OF FREDERICK
CARDER EARLY THIS
CENTURY. VASE AT LEFT
IS OF AURENE, ACID-
ETCHED IN BLUE AND
GREEN. ONE AT RIGHT
WITH DOMED FOOT IS
AURENE (GOLDEN) WITH
GOLD, GREEN, AND WHITE
VINE DECORATION. VASE
AT LEFT IS 28.4 CENTI-
METERS HIGH. *The Corn-
ing Museum of Glass,
Corning Glass Center,
Corning, New York.*

BOWL BY EMIL J. LAR-
SON, DURAND GLASS
WORKS, VINELAND, NEW
JERSEY, CA. 1920–30.
OF CLEAR GLASS, THIS
WAS FREE-BLOWN WITH
THREAD DECORATION OF
RED AND OPAQUE WHITE
THREADS. *The Corning
Museum of Glass, Corn-
ing Glass Center, Corn-
ing, New York.*

GRASSHOPPERS ON LONG STEMS
ADORN THIS VASE OF GREEN SEMI-
OPAQUE GLASS. *Author's collection.*

"KEW-BLAS" FOOTED
BOWL MADE BY UNION
GLASS WORKS OF
SOMERVILLE, MASSA-
CHUSETTS, ABOUT 1900.
NAME "KEW-BLAS"
MARKED ON BASE IS AN
ANAGRAM OF THE NAME
W. S. BLAKE, WHO WAS
COMPANY'S GENERAL
MANAGER. *The Corning
Museum of Glass, Corn-
ing Glass Center, Corn-
ing, New York.*

Val St. Lambert factory in Belgium, and the bulk of these were reminiscent of Gallé's Art Nouveau work.

Imitating Tiffany iridescent wares was the Bohemian company of J. Lötz Witwe, and these wares, frequently referred to by collectors as Loetz, are currently available but generally at prices considerably below those being paid for Tiffany pieces. Some of this glass is marked with the name "Loetz," but numerous pieces are found unsigned.

Glass in the Art Nouveau manner was produced as late as the First World War, when it was superseded by a more functional type of glass.

Although vases and other decorative objects of outstanding Art Nouveau glass presently bring high prices, there are still available literally thousands of small gas and electric light shades in this style at prices of $35 and under, though some recently have brought as much as $45 and $50.

In his *American Art Nouveau Glass,* Albert Christian Revi, who has established himself as a ranking authority on art glass in general, illustrates a wide array of Art Nouveau lamps and lamp shades offered by such firms as the U. S. Art Bent Glass Company, Inc., of Hartford, Connecticut; the H. J. Peters Company of Chicago, Illinois; the Frankel Light Company of Cleveland, Ohio; the Cincinnati Artistic Wrought Iron Works of Cincinnati, Ohio; and the Albert Sechrist Manufacturing Company of Denver, Colorado.

In glass, certainly, Art Nouveau found its prime expression in ornament, but the bodies of the vessels and other objects also were ornamental in themselves, often characterized by an undulating grace that invariably carried the strong suggestion of movement.

III

Art Nouveau Pottery

Art Nouveau porcelain vases, signed, "Paris-Louchet." The hair of the nude figures is done in gold paint. These are fine examples of High Art Nouveau. Signatures are on the bases. *Lightner Museum, St. Augustine, Florida.*

Both Tiffany and Gallé, primary exponents of Art Nouveau in glass, also produced some extraordinary examples of pottery in the same style, but the aggregate output, by comparison with the glass, was small.

Tiffany's pottery, as his glass, was designated Favrile. Some of it was cast in molds and some was thrown on the potter's wheel. Many Tiffany pottery vases were patterned in form after flowers or plants. Decorations, also, were usually floral and were customarily relief designs, molded in the clay. The color was derived from the clay rather than by extraneous means.

Because Tiffany Favrile pottery was made as one-of-a-kind pieces, it is scarce today. Some pottery vases were designed to serve as lamp bases. Colors included ivory, various shades of green, brown, and yellow, and a pure white. Glazes were produced in gold luster, bronze, buff, green, purple, and other hues. Sometimes pottery was combined with metal, and porcelain—now and then with pottery ornamentation—and was used for some of the bases. Each pottery item had the initials L.C.T. incised in its base. Unglazed pottery was also made, and the company would sometimes coat unglazed objects with a thin film of copper or bronze.

Tiffany himself had long admired Chinese porcelains, and perhaps it was this admiration that induced him to experiment with pottery and porcelain himself. Perhaps, too, he may have been impressed by the successes of the Rookwood Pottery, of Cincinnati, Ohio, whose productions, incidentally, were sold by Tiffany & Company. At any rate, when he did enter this field, his primary concern was with form, decoration, and color, and he was influenced in these areas by his preoccupation with new interpretations of the Art Nouveau style.

Most of the Tiffany work with pottery was undertaken shortly after the outbreak of the First World War. His 1915 catalogue advised that Tiffany Favrile pottery was then being manufactured in table lamps, vases, jars, and other pieces with "artistic effects entirely different from anything heretofore shown." [1] Favrile bronze pottery was offered at prices ranging from $10 to $200.

In addition to vases and lamp bases, Favrile pottery was made in the form of inkwells, boxes, jardinieres, ashtrays, and tiles. At the Parke-Bernet auction sales of art objects in Laurelton Hall held September 24 through 28, 1946, five small Favrile pottery vases glazed to simulate marble and ranging in height from 3½ to 6¼ inches were sold at a lot for only $35.

Favrile pottery vases were made in numerous sizes, ranging from only about 2 to more than 20 inches tall, and in forms that included ovoid, cylindrical, quadrangular, globular, baluster, oval, melon, double-gourd, and pear shapes. A few were made in the form of blossoms.

Émile Gallé had experimented with pottery before turning to glass, and some of the early pieces anticipate his Art Nouveau style, featuring an organic form. Many of his pottery objects are asymmetrical in form with their decoration following suit.

He turned out plates, bowls, teapots (some in shapes that are little short of fantastic), ashtrays, and, of course, vases. Colors were obviously a prime concern, and one often encounters on Gallé pottery bold and striking colors rather than the paler hues and pastels normally associated with Art Nouveau. The ornamentation itself merges with the very

GREEN GLAZED PIERCED POTTERY
VASE BY JOHN D. WAREHAM, 1901,
PRODUCED BY ROOKWOOD POTTERY
COMPANY. THE VASE IS 7½ INCHES
HIGH. *Collection, The Museum of
Modern Art, New York City, Phyllis
B. Lambert Fund.*

EWER IN POTTERY FROM THE ROOK-
WOOD POTTERY COMPANY OF CIN-
CINNATI, OHIO, IS TYPICAL OF THAT
COMPANY'S FINE WARES. *Lightner
Museum, St. Augustine, Florida.*

structure of the pottery objects. When plant forms are used for decoration, those selected are exotic, not the commonplace flowers and plants found in the typical nursery or florist's shop.

Gallé pottery has so far been almost completely neglected in the multitude of books that have appeared about pottery. Since Gallé was primarily in the category of a "studio" potter, no references will be found to him or his wares in books of marks. Nevertheless, his pottery is now sought after by a relatively small but discriminating group of collectors, and prices ranging in the hundreds of dollars have been paid for some pieces. Its appreciation appears inevitable in the future.

The Rookwood Pottery, founded in 1880 in Cincinnati through the energetic efforts of Mrs. Maria Longworth Nichols, became the ranking art pottery in the United States and maintained that position for nearly four decades. A number of times during its existence it changed management but finally, in the 1950's, found itself unable to compete with mass production methods and prices. The business was purchased by the Herschede Hall Clock Company in late 1959, and the operations were moved the following year to Starkville, Mississippi, where they were finally closed down altogether in 1967.

In the 1890's, Rookwood turned to the Art Nouveau style. Scores of vases with floral motifs so beloved of Art Nouveau artists and artisans were produced by Rookwood. Some of the flowers were stylized and were depicted in conjunction with long, flowing stems and convolvular leaves. Flowers used for design on Rookwood pieces included chrysanthemums, iris, milkweed, lilies, clover, the night blooming cereus, pansies, poppies, wistaria, bleeding hearts, roses, orchids, tulips, jonquils, cornflowers, and the jack-in-the-pulpit. Other naturalistic elements used in decoration embraced dragonflies, pine cones, teasel, blackberry and cherry blossoms, fish, storks, grapes, mushrooms, dogwood blossoms, cyclamen, ivy, mistletoe, geese, and even spiders. Most floral designs were painted under the glaze, and many of the naturalistic elements were presented conventionally so that there is a definite line of demarcation between the Art Nouveau and the traditional styles in Rookwood pieces.

One pattern in Rookwood's Vellum—a transparent matte glaze—featured a conventional dragonfly but with a long, curving tail that bore close kinship to Art Nouveau's whiplash line.

A number of candlesticks and lamps were made in flower form, including those of the lily and the tulip. One striking production was an electrolier in twin tulip form; the heart of each tulip was designed to hold a light socket and bulb. One also encounters chocolate pots, teapots, and cream and sugar sets decorated with clover, the stems of which were long and undulating. Such stems also supported mushrooms that provided the decorative motif for both chocolate and tea pots in the Iris ware developed by Rookwood in the mid-1890's and characterized by sunny tones in pastel colors on backgrounds that were often blue or gray.

Rookwood's Sea Green wares also appear to have had their inspiration in Art Nouveau motifs, some of these decorated with fish marvelously transparent in their watery environment.

Various marks were used to identify Rookwood pottery through the years, the first standard mark having been the name of the pottery itself in capital letters of a block-like character accompanied by the year of production. Other types of marks had been utilized with some inconsistency earlier.

The widely recognized "RP" monogram was inaugurated in 1886 and is familiar to all collectors of this ware. A year later a flame point was placed atop this monogram, and thereafter, until 1900, one additional flame mark was added to designate the year of production. From 1901, this monogram with 14 flame marks (designating the year 1900) was continued with the addition below the monogram of a Roman numeral used to designate the year. These various marks and also the marks and initials of decorators will be found in several books on Rookwood pottery written in recent years.

The beauty of glaze and design of many Rookwood pieces has long been recognized by collectors with the result that the finer pieces have been and continue to be eagerly sought. Prices, therefore, are on the rise. Not long ago a rare Rookwood vase, standing 42 inches tall and made in two parts, was advertised for sale at a price of $3,500. The vase was dated 1892 and, said the advertiser, was marked "S" for special. Such prices, however, are the exception, not the rule, and many fine Rookwood pieces may still be found for under $50, smaller ones at $25 and less.

Both in this country and abroad, Rookwood has been judged meritorious enough to be included in a number of museums. The pottery boasted many extraordinarily talented decorators and artists, some of whom were internationally known. Among them were the attorney-artist E. P. Cranch, of Cincinnati; Artus Van Briggle, who left to establish his own art pottery; Albert R. Valentien, who was in charge of the decorating department during the pottery's early years; his wife, Anna Marie Valentien; Laura A. Fry, who subsequently became associated with the Lonhuda Pottery in Steubenville, Ohio; and Kataro Shirayamadani, the Japanese artist who developed many new Rookwood shapes. The Cincinnati Art Museum has preserved many of the finest early Rookwood examples, originally acquired by that city's Women's Art Museum Association.

The total production of the Rookwood pottery during its existence was tremendous. The collector who is investment-minded, however, should seek the finest pieces he can. Although vases were turned out in the largest quantities, the pottery also made such articles as pots for chocolate and tea, cups and saucers, lamps, candlesticks, dinnerwares, and other utilitarian and decorative objects. Generally, although not invariably, pieces signed by the artist bring the higher prices. A listing of artists and decorators, together with brief biographical sketches, may be found in *The Book of Rookwood Pottery* by Herbert Peck, and in other books and articles, some of which are listed in the Selected Bibliography. Unfortunately, some people believe that certain Rookwood pieces marked with an "X" on the bottom are special. In a way, they are: the "X" was used to denote inferior pieces known as "seconds" in the trade.

A number of striking Art Nouveau designs were created by Van Briggle, who was a protégé of Mrs. Maria Longworth Nichols and who, after working at Rookwood from 1887 to 1899, left because of poor health to open his own studio pottery in Colorado Springs, Colorado. Through the help of Mrs. Nichols and her pottery, Van Briggle studied art in Italy and also in Paris, where one of his teachers was Benjamin Constant (1845–1902), the distinguished French portrait painter. While abroad, Van Briggle came in contact with the Art Nouveau movement, which made a profound impression upon him.

When he returned to this country and resumed work at Rookwood, he experimented with solid glazes and with colors, seeking to extend the range of those then in general use. After establishing his own pottery in Colorado, he continued his experiments, perfecting a matte glaze and turning out a number of pieces for the commercial market in late 1901. The productions met with acclaim, not only from connoisseurs but in several of the art periodicals, so that an expansion of the small works was justified.

In 1902, Artus Van Briggle married Anne Gregory, an artist in her own right, and she joined him in his work with pottery. Two years later, at the peak of his career and when his creations were being heralded both in this country and abroad, Artus Van Briggle died at 33.

A number of major Van Briggle pieces were strictly Art Nouveau, including a vase he named "Lorelei"; one entitled

"Lady of the Lily," depicting a languid nude on an asymmetrical calla lily vase form; a footed flower bowl, "Siren of the Sea," graced by a mermaid; and a remarkably beautiful vase form, "Despondency," with a finely modeled female nude with flowing hair at her top. "Despondency," was ultimately acquired by the Louvre at a record price of $3,000.[2]

After Van Briggle's death, the pottery was reorganized and officially designated the Van Briggle Company with his widow as its president. A few years later the physical plant was considerably expanded and its production widened to include architectural type decorative pieces.

Van Briggle's Art Nouveau creations are characterized by fine modeling and distinctive hues of color, as well as curved forms and decoration that includes not only the languid female figure but foliage, flowers, trees, and insects created in low relief.

Many of the early Van Briggle pieces were produced by means of molds, but in varying glazes and glaze treatments. Air brushes were used to apply the matte finish.

The Van Briggle Pottery continues in operation today, having changed names and management several times after the founder's death, and copies of orginal Van Briggle models have been reproduced. The productions are identified by conjoined A's inside a square, incised, and, in the cases of productions after about 1920, the name "Van Briggle," sometimes with "U.S.A." added. (During the first few years of this century, artists used certain Roman numerals to identify their pieces. Some also signed either their initials or full names.)

Within the past two or three years, an interest in the early Van Briggle productions has intensified, but many objects are still available at relatively low prices, and a number have recently been advertised at under $20.

Mrs. Bogue's *The Van Briggle Story,* published late in 1968, presents much of the history of Artus Van Briggle and

WELLER'S LOUWELSA FLORAL VASE SIGNED WITH ARTIST'S INITIALS, "W. H." DONE IN MAHAGONY, BROWN, YELLOW, ORANGE, AND RUST COLORS. VASE IS 11 INCHES HIGH. *Collection of Mr. and Mrs. M. D. Cole.*

LOUWELSA WELLER VASE WAS PRODUCED IN ZANESVILLE, OHIO, EARLY IN THIS CENTURY. WELLER POTTERY IS ATTRACTING AN INCREASING NUMBER OF COLLECTORS. *Mr. and Mrs. C. C. Pritchard, The Golden Peacock, St. Augustine, Florida.*

LOUWELSA WELLER VASE SIGNED BY "ABEL." DECOR IS THREE FLYING BIRDS. ARTIST UTILIZED MAHAGONY, GREEN, YELLOW, RUST, AND ORANGE COLORS. THIS WARE WAS MADE FROM 1895 TO 1918. *Collection of Mr. and Mrs. M. D. Cole.*

the pottery he established. An excellent short study was also written for *Western Collector* by Ralph E. Bayer in 1969.

Several other potteries in Ohio ranked as competitors to Rookwood and Van Briggle. The best-known were the Lonhuda Pottery, established in Steubenville, Ohio, by W. A. Long and two associates; the Samuel A. Weller Pottery, originally founded in Fultonham and moved to Zanesville, Ohio, in 1892 (and at which W. A. Long was employed for a while); J. B. Owens Pottery Company, which made pottery in Zanesville (and which also, at one period, employed the services of W. A. Long); and the Roseville Pottery Company, formed in 1892 and moved to Zanesville six years later.

Weller, Owens, and Roseville all produced some Art Nouveau wares as well as various other types, and publicity about these companies in the past few years has brought them to collectors' attention. Weller, with Long's help, made Lonhuda pottery, which Long had originally produced and which closely resembled one of the Rookwood types in glaze and color. Subsequently, the Lonhuda name was changed to Louwelsa, this line being produced until shortly after the outbreak of the First World War in Europe. Both Lonhuda and Louwelsa offered some Art Nouveau naturalistic motifs, primarily flowers, vines, and leaves.

Weller's Aurelian ware, decorated in tones of red, brown, and yellow and introduced during the first decade of this century, also featured Art Nouveau designs. And soft Art Nouveau hues (grays, browns, and a reddish pink) characterized the company's Eocean line, which often featured floral motifs. Particularly Art Nouveau in character was Weller's Sicardo, featuring a metallic luster created by a French artist, Jacques Sicard, with the help of an assistant and produced for about five years from 1902 to 1907. The luster was mildly reminiscent of Tiffany's sheens and so were the flowing lines of some of Sicardo's forms.

However, Weller also created a line specifically named L'Art Nouveau with semi-matte relief decoration and featur-

Buffalo Pottery Company plate, early twentieth century.

ing hues of green and pink. Louise and Evan Purviance and Norris F. Schneider in a color plate book on Zanesville Art pottery report that the L'Art Nouveau line was produced in 1903 and 1904.[3] Until his doors were closed in 1948, Weller introduced numerous lines of pottery, and these are listed in the book just mentioned, which also presents capsule histories of the various potteries that flourished in the Zanesville area and displays many examples of their pieces in color.

In addition to vases, the Weller company made jardinieres, clock cases, bowls, pitchers and ewers, jars, bonbon dishes, jewel boxes, lamp bases, candlesticks, mugs, birds and animals, and a variety of novelties.

Similarly, the J. B. Owens Pottery Company turned out Art Nouveau pieces, particularly in wares coated with metallic colors and called Opalesce and Feroza. This company manufactured art pottery in Zanesville from 1891 to 1907.

Roseville Pottery Company's art wares were developed under the supervision of Ross C. Purdy, who was employed at the opening of this century and first turned out a line he called Rozane, a good many pieces of which were decorated with floral motifs and covered with a brownish glaze. These pieces are marked with the trade name of the ware, the earliest ones having the addition "R. P. Co."

Several variations of the Rozane line were developed, including Rozane Royal, Rozane Mongol, Rozane Mara, Rozane Egypto, and Rozane Woodland. Some of the Rozane Mara is peculiarly Art Nouveau in shape. As was the case with Weller, Roseville also introduced a wide variety of types until its closing in 1954. Many pieces of Roseville were marked with labels, but the use of the impressed mark "Roseville U.S.A." started at about the time of the Depression.

The color plate book mentioned earlier is recommended to those who want to view a variety of the wares of these Zanesville potteries in their original colors. Mr. Schneider, incidentally, was a pioneer in researching the Zanesville plants and published a most informative booklet, *Zanesville Art Pottery,* in 1963.

Creations of the Buffalo Pottery, organized in Buffalo, New York, in 1901 by the Larkin Company—originally a soap manufacturing firm that branched out to become a major diversified mail-order business, thanks in part, at least, to the promotional efforts of Elbert Hubbard, who subsequently was to found the Roycroft Corporation—are just beginning to experience a surge in value.

A group of pitchers strongly influenced by the Art Nouveau style was made by Buffalo Pottery for several years, beginning in 1905. These had underglaze decorations and were semi-vitreous wares (vitrified wares were not produced by this company until 1915).

In 1908 Buffalo introduced a line of pottery it named Deldare, and these pieces are more eagerly sought by today's collectors than any other of the company's lines. Witness the number of advertisements that have appeared in the past few years in the various collector periodicals offering pieces in this line for sale or seeking pieces. Delightful decorative scenes, many patterned after book illustrations, are utilized on the Deldare pieces. Among the best-known are the Fallowfield Hunt illustrations, originally created by the English artist Cecil C. W. Aldin. Aldin illustrated several books, among them *The Romance of the Road,* illustrated with charming coaching scenes and wayside inns, which now command good prices in the rare book market. Buffalo also utilized other English scenes, and its Deldare pieces bear not only the scenes but their captions.

Some time after the introduction of the Deldare line, Buffalo inaugurated a line it called Emerald Deldare, but its production period was brief, although the pottery did continue its Deldare line after the end of the First World War. Emerald Deldare was decorated by the use of transfer prints —a method long employed by other potteries throughout the world—which were hand-decorated and then glazed. The borders utilized on Emerald Deldare assign it to the Art Nouveau tradition, some incorporating such naturalistic elements as sinuous leaves and flowers. Others were made in the

PORCELAIN VASE BY ROXENBURG, THE HAGUE, CA. 1900. *Courtesy, Victoria and Albert Museum, London.*

geometric style that derived primarily from Germany and Austria. A considerable number featured scenes from the *Dr. Syntax* series after Thomas Rowlandson, the famous English caricaturist, whose illustrations for *Dr. Syntax's Three Tours*, written by William Combe and originally published in the early nineteenth century in London, are among his best-known works. Emerald Deldare is identified by the name on pieces in this line, together with the name of the pottery. Pieces of it are bringing relatively high prices today.

Other pottery and porcelain manufacturers also turned out articles in the Art Nouveau style, some by design, others by coincidence, and some pieces were made by small studio potters. And, of course, literally vast quantities of pottery that feature asymmetry in form and decor have been fashioned since the latter part of the nineteenth century, but the majority were created not under the influence of Art Nouveau per se but under the direct influence of the Japanese style, which in itself had such a profound impact upon Art Nouveau.

Among the art potteries abroad that produced some pieces in the Art Nouveau style was the Southall Pottery, operated by the Martin brothers in England. Edwin Martin, the designer among the four brothers, devised ornamentation that featured foliage and flowers, shells, and sea creatures, including anemones, crabs, and jellyfish.

Also in England, the Linthorpe Pottery made a few articles that anticipated Art Nouveau, articles designed by Christopher Dresser, its gifted and versatile art director, who also during his career was an architect, furniture and fabric designer, and author.

Several small German potters contributed to the Art Nouveau style, imbuing creations with the *Jugendstil* spirit. Among them were Johann J. Scharvogel and Max Laeuger. Fairly late in the movement, some pottery in the Sezession style, featuring rather simple forms with a tendency toward the rectilinear and the geometrical appeared in Austria. Some Art Nouveau pottery is found bearing the name Roxenburg, made in The Hague.

Although some work was achieved under the influence of the new style by Marc Louis Solon in England and at the Sèvres, Meissen, Copenhagen, and Rörstrand factories and also in England by Doulton and Minton, the major pottery and porcelain manufacturers preferred to stick with traditional forms for the bulk of their output. Even so, and although Art Nouveau pottery and porcelain are not even mentioned in the majority of books dealing with the ceramic art, a surprisingly large number of potteries did produce at least some pieces in the new style, as a reexamination of the output of the 1890's and early 1900's will reveal.

The Art Nouveau designs of Solon, who went to Minton's from Sèvres, executed in *pâte-sur-pâte* are in great demand today and at comparatively high prices, since such wares were expensive to make originally. Their decoration was achieved by painting in successive coatings of fluid slip (thinned clay), which required both skill and labor, after which the pieces were fired, the glaze applied, and the pieces fired a second time. Despite their cost, *pâte-sur-pâte* pieces are still available today at prices that are not greatly above the original cost, and these could prove an excellent investment. M. L. Solon, father of Leon Victor Solon, worked using acid-etching and other techniques that somewhat speeded the execution of pieces.

Within the past year a number of dealers, recognizing the Art Nouveau form and decoration, have discovered and advertised Art Nouveau pottery and porcelain made by both domestic and foreign potteries. Nevertheless, until greater attention is focused once again on the new art, the collector still has an opportunity to stumble across "sleepers" on antiques shops shelves.

IV

Art Nouveau Jewelry

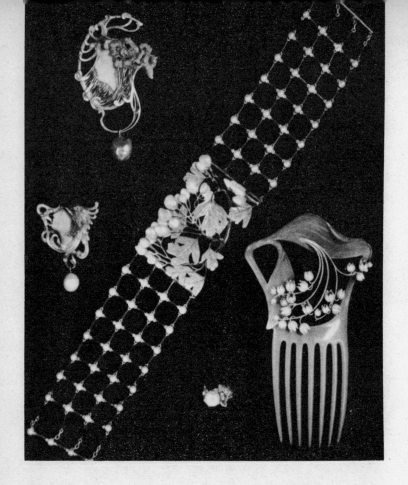

Here are several interesting creations in jewelry by René Lalique. Pendant in chiseled gold, white stone, baroque pearls, enameled is seen at top left, and below this is a gold-enameled brooch with baroque pearls, signed. Across the center is a dog collar, gold, enameled, and with baroque pearls, signed. The small ring below is of chiseled gold with a pearl and is signed and dated 1900. The comb at right below is of sculptured horn, gold-enameled, and also signed and dated 1900. *Courtesy, Musée des Arts Décoratifs, Paris.*

THE MOST PROMINENT NAME in the field of Art Nouveau jewelry is René Lalique, who also produced glass in this style. Lalique, born in 1860, bears a kinship, distant though it may seem, to Peter Carl Fabergé, that extraordinary goldsmith and jeweler to the Imperial Court of Russia. Both men were innovators, endowed with great creative talent and an extraordinary sense of beauty.

Lalique, as we have already noted, began his career as an independent artisan creating jewelry for established businesses, before entering the employment of well-known jewelry establishments and, in 1920, founding his own business. As was the case with other leading Art Nouveau craftsmen, Lalique rebelled against the traditional and used precious and semiprecious stones and other substances to fashion jewelry and costume accessories that are recognized today as prime examples of Art Nouveau.

The value of jewelry is largely dependent, of course, upon its components. Diamonds are more highly valued than moonstones; the emerald ranks far above the carnelian. But Lalique combined the gemstone with the semiprecious stone or with such substances as horn to create decorative articles that recently have commanded prices well above the actual value of the materials themselves.

Like the majority of other Art Nouveau artists, Lalique preferred pale hues, often utilizing pearls, moonstones, mother-of-pearl, semitransparent horn, and other stones and substances with delicate hues of color rather than such flamboyant gems as rubies and sapphires.

HAIR ORNAMENT OF METAL AND CUT AND ENAMELED CRYSTAL, SIGNED LALIQUE (BEFORE 1900). *Courtesy, Musée des Arts Décoratifs, Paris.*

LALIQUE BROOCH OF GLASS MOUNTED IN GILDED SILVER, ABOUT 1910. *Courtesy, Musée des Arts Décoratifs, Paris.*

Lalique, apparently more fascinated by irregularity of shape than by the brilliance or beauty of the stones or by their rarity, chose those with an asymmetrical structure to create jewelry in asymmetrical forms. Illustrated in *Art at Auction 1966–67* is a Lalique tiara set with diamonds and fashioned in the shape of fern leaves that brought $700 at auction at Sotheby's in London in 1967.[1]

He created many ornaments, ranging from brooches to combs, in designs that employed leaves, blossoms, and plants, some of which seem to convey a sense of writhing motion. His pieces bore little or no kinship to the traditional forms of jewelry or ornament. And in some, such as an outstanding and large brooch he designed in 1900, he incorporated the female head with flowing locks.

Lalique did not produce inexpensive trinkets or baubles that could be purchased for a few dollars at the neighborhood jewelry store. Because his pieces were individually crafted and required consummate skill and the exercise of a high degree of artistic imagination, their primary appeal originally was to those who could afford jewelry at its finest.

Lalique began designing jewelry when he was barely out of his teens. After serving for awhile as a freelance designer with considerable success, he joined the staff of the fashionable Parisian firm of Chez de Stape; then, a few years later, he opened a studio, where once again he accepted commission assignments from leading French jewelry establishments. Of particular interest was his work with horn instead of the tortoise shell as a background for his mountings of jewel stones.

Even in an era when mass production was well under way, Lalique chose the path of the individual craftsman. Each piece he created was unique; each was fashioned solely by his own hands. At the age of 25, he won recognition with an exhibition at the Salon des Artistes Français, which led to new commissions for him by distinguished and wealthy clients.

Because he eschewed mass production, Lalique's jewelry is not abundant, but available items are being avidly sought

PENDANT, CHISELED GOLD, WHITE STONE, BAROQUE PEARL, ENAMELED, SIGNED LALIQUE, 1900. *Courtesy, Musée des Arts Décoratifs, Paris.*

RENÉ LALIQUE PENDANT AND CHAIN MADE OF GOLD, DIAMONDS, AND GLASS. *The Metropolitan Museum of Art, gift of Miss Mary F. Failing, 1944, offered in memory of Henrietta Ellison Failing.*

today by astute collectors, not only for their own striking beauty but also as a hedge against the inflationary tide that is shrinking the value of savings and many other forms of financial investment.

Some splendid Art Nouveau jewelry was also created around the turn of the century by the Englishman Charles Robert Ashbee, who was primarily an architect and designer. He crafted a number of silver pieces, of which several were plated with gold. Ashbee's designs often embodied the new style's curvilinear elements. In addition, he conceived designs for articles of silver.

Ashbee's jewelry was made under his personal supervision at the Guild and School of Handicraft in London's East End. Though his designs were based on nature, they were imbued with the curvilinear characteristics of Art Nouveau. Most of his objects were of silver, often in conjunction with jewels, including amethyst, amber, and pearl. There is evidence, too, that he was influenced by the remarkable Benvenuto Cellini, whose work he edited for publication in the latter part of the last century, but the influence seems to have been largely on his careful and meticulous workmanship.

Among the other outstanding British designers of jewelry in the Art Nouveau manner were David Veazey, Fred Robinson, Mr. and Mrs. Arthur Gaskin, who worked as a husband-and-wife team, J. Herbert McNair and his wife, Frances, Edgar Simpson, who worked in Nottingham, Talwyn Morris, who used aluminum, Archibald Knox, and several other women who attained some prominence in the field, among them the Misses Annie McLeish, Winifred Hodgkinson, E. Larcombe, Ethel M. Hodgkinson, Katie Fisher, and Edith Pickett.

In France, meanwhile, in addition to Lalique, jewelry creations of importance were achieved by Eugène Grasset working in collaboration with M. Véver, Georges Fouquet, Eugène Colonna, Maurice Dufrène, Paul Follet, Marcel Bing, the painter Victor Prouvé, Paul Richard, Charles Rivaud, and Jules Desbois.

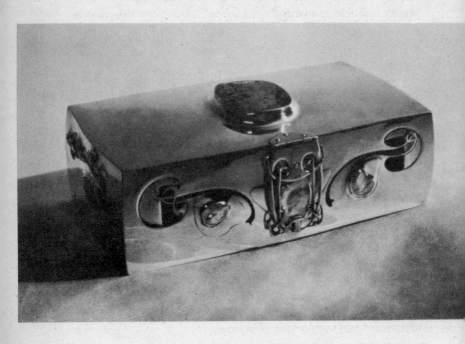

JEWEL BOX OF SILVER, MOTHER-OF-PEARL, TURQUOISE, AND ENAMEL, DESIGNED BY ARCHIBALD KNOX AND MADE BY LIBERTY AND COMPANY IN ENGLAND ABOUT 1900. THE BOX MEASURES 11¼ BY 6 BY 3¼ INCHES IN SIZE. *Collection, The Museum of Modern Art, New York City, gift of the family of Mrs. John D. Rockefeller.*

In Belgium, jewelers of note included Paul Dubois, Henri van de Velde (who attained greater distinction in other fields), and Philip Wolfers. And in Germany a leading creator of Art Nouveau jewelry was William Lucas von Cranach.

Other artists, craftsmen, and designers who worked in the new style also designed occasional pieces of jewelry. Some of these men and women appear to have been multifaceted geniuses: painters often took up ceramics, architects frequently designed furniture for the homes or other establishments they built or turned to sculpture, ceramicists, such as Gallé, also worked with glass and furniture, and so on.

As in the case of glass and pottery, much Art Nouveau jewelry utilized insects and plant life in its design. The materials chosen were not selected because of the intrinsic value of the substance itself, but because of a subtlety of color that adapted itself well to this new style. Some of the finest Art Nouveau jewelry bore a striking kinship with sculpture in miniature, as has been pointed out by Greta Daniel in her chapter on the decorative arts in *Art Nouveau: Art and Design at the Turn of the Century,* a book mentioned earlier. Jewelry also permitted the designer to let his fantasy range free and to shape some designs that appealed to feeling rather than to intellect.

Commercial versions of Art Nouveau jewelry appeared in the United States not long after 1900, and before the end of the first decade, these were being produced in profusion and great variety. These commercial pieces continued to be made until about the time of World War 1, when design deteriorated rapidly. Numerous producers were content simply to adapt designs created by competitors or to use the same or quite similar designs on different forms of jewelry.

Commercial Art Nouveau was extended to finger rings, costume pins of all kinds, charms, lockets, belt buckles, festoon chains, sleeve buttons, bracelets, and, of course, to scores of jewelry boxes and cases.

Decorative motifs included flowers, vines, female heads

with languid expressions and flowing locks, insects of various families, especially butterflies and bees, mermaids, stalks, seahorses, and the whiplash element.

Designers of jewelry and accessories for personal adornment found themselves, in many instances, torn between an affection for Art Nouveau and a predeliction for the rococo—with some extraordinary results. Designs that were strictly Art Nouveau in character are found embraced in an overall framework of shells, scrolls, and foliage arranged in a studiously asymmetrical fashion. The rococo style, which flourished in Europe between 1735 and 1765, was revived by commercial designers late in the nineteenth century, and those who followed in their wake through the First World War could not or would not try to shake off the shackles. Whether the results of this union should properly be termed watered-down Art Nouveau, degraded rococo, or plain bastard, if you'll forgive the phrase, is debatable. Nevertheless, we will include a good many articles of this type in this book under a sort of poetic license sometimes appropriated by writers on art and antiques. Much Art Nouveau was influenced by the rococo, sometimes strongly.

The truth seems to be that the first two decades of the present century were indolent years for creative designers, who found it much simpler to copy or adapt than to create. Of course, there were exceptions, some of whom we have already mentioned and others who will be introduced in the pages that follow.

One will also find among the jewelry produced early in this century designs that obviously started out to be Art Nouveau surrounded by symmetrical elements or set off against one another in symmetrical fashion. The lady with the flowing locks is found abundantly on all sorts of pieces from stickpins to brooches. Sometimes her expression is languid, as perhaps it should be, but more often it is vapid—and sometimes frankly stupid. Occasionally the lady appears full length, clad in some diaphanous garment from loins to toes but with bare upper torso. Occasionally, too, her hair is adorned with flowers.

THESE LOCKETS WERE ADVERTISED BETWEEN 1905 AND 1907. ONES AT LEFT AND AT RIGHT IN TOP ROW HAD TURQUOISE SETTINGS; THE FIRST TWO FROM LEFT IN SECOND ROW WERE SET WITH BRILLIANTS AS WAS THE ONE AT LEFT IN BOTTOM ROW.

It was the floral element, however, that obsessed the commerical Art Nouveau jewelry designers. One constantly encounters lilies, roses, daisies, tulips, carnations, and others, often with long, flowing stems and tendrils, which sometimes form a part of the border of the article itself. Among the more delightful pieces are those shaped as flowers with unfolded petals. These were used as stickpins, hatpins, brooches, sleeve buttons, chatelette pins, and other types of clothing pins.

Just returning to popularity are the small lockets, made of sterling silver, gold, or gold-filling, much favored by the ladies at the outset of this century and worn attached by a chain or a chatelaine. Picture lockets, which usually open at the top by means of a clasp and into which either one or two pictures can be inserted, are especially in demand at the present time. They often are set with small precious stones, other types of stone, or a combination of the two.

Gold lockets set with precious stones and featuring the asymmetrical Art Nouveau shape with floral designs were in particular vogue during the first of this century. One set with a single diamond and a ruby and with a floral design was tendered in 1907 at a wholesale price of $22.50. A somewhat similar one set with a single diamond and with space for two pictures bore a wholesale price of $15.25.

On the other hand, there were scores of less expensive lockets, some set with brilliants, that wholesaled at prices ranging from only $2 to about $7. Some were gold filled, others were of sterling silver. Decoration was by embossing —that is, with the designs raised in relief.

The brooch seemed almost universally popular during the heyday of Art Nouveau. Between 1905 and 1910, thousands were made in the new style. An especially intriguing one incorporated a woman's head to form one side, her long locks flowing out in two directions to form the remainder of the brooch, and joined together by a bunch of grapes and leaves. Made of sterling silver, it wholesaled in 1905 for $14.

SOLID GOLD AND GOLD-FILLED BROOCHES OF 1904–7 PERIOD WERE CRE-
ATED IN THE NEW ART STYLE AND WERE TURNED OUT BY THE THOUSANDS.

Others were formed of a framework of intertwined flowers, leaves, and stems. One of these, set with a sapphire and pearls, was offered at a wholesale price of $15.50, another with an opal and pearls at $10, and one with a ruby and pearls at $12.50

Gold-filled brooches set with brilliants and small pearls or with brilliants alone could be bought at retail during the first decade of the twentieth century in a price range of $2.50 to about $10. Some of the designs were outlandish, but others were quite good. These brooches are cropping up now in the antique shops, and you'll have to be your own judge of what is good and what is mediocre.

Dealers report a fairly brisk demand at the present time for bracelets, particularly gold ones, although gold-filled bracelets also are being bought as costume pieces. Floral designs in the Art Nouveau manner arranged as bracelet fronts were produced in the early 1900's, as were a good many medium-to-wide band bracelets with floral designs around the entire exterior. Gold engraved bracelets of good quality could be purchased in the early 1900's at prices of about $30 and up, some of the better ones retailing for $65 to $100.

Of course, too, many gold-filled bracelets were made to sell in a moderate price range of around $2.50 to $10. One with a ruby center and four French pearls was available in 1907 for less than $7. A fairly large percentage of the bracelets were adjustable. The Art Nouveau designs on many of them are interesting and, if these pieces are not of great value, they still make excellent gifts for teen-age girls.

Belt buckles and sash pins may make a comeback when the intriguing variety in which they were produced is more adequately recognized. Many belt pins that are strictly Art Nouveau still linger from early in the century. Sash pins with sterling silver fronts and embossed designs were wholesaling in 1906 for as little as $15 a dozen, and 14-karat gold-filled ones, some with baroque pearls, were offered in jobbers' catalogues at $19.50 to $31.20 a dozen. Some pins and buckles

ART NOUVEAU BELT PINS
WITH STERLING SILVER FRONTS.
THESE WHOLESALED IN 1907
AT $15 A DOZEN.

GOLD-FILLED SASH BUCKLE
SET WITH A RUBY-COLORED
STONE DATES IN FIRST DECADE
OF THIS CENTURY.

TYPICAL ART NOUVEAU JEW-
ELRY BOX OF THE FIRST DEC-
ADE OF THIS CENTURY. IT
CAME BOTH GOLD-PLATED AND
SILVER-LINED AND RETAILED
FOR UNDER $10.

COMBINATION NECK CHAIN
AND CHATELAINE PIN IN GOLD
WITH EIGHT PEARLS. CA. 1906.

had solid fronts, others had cutout designs. Relatively few
such buckles and pins have made their way into dealers'
showcases, but so many were originally produced that quantities of them are likely to be found stashed away somewhere
in older homes, perhaps among the effects of your grandmothers or great-grandmothers.

Various other types of pins, from lace pins to hatpins (and
also stickpins for both men and women) as well as chains
and fobs were designed in the new style. Neck chains had
Art Nouveau chatelaine pins at one end. When ladies wore
very small watches on their blouses, these were often attached
to either chatelaines or small link chains that pinned at one
end of the blouse. A lady's "safety fob" linked to the end of
one such chain made in 1907 and featuring a damsel with
flowing locks and flowers in her hair in brooch form was
listed in a wholesalers' catalogue as having been manufactured by "S.O.B. & Co." Such safety fobs and also vest chains
for men were turned out in profusion in the days before the
blouse and the pocket watch succumbed to the wristwatch.

Hatpins have been collected for years, and there are some
intriguing ones available in the Art Nouveau manner. The
terminal of one type of pin was a lady's head with that
eternally flowing hair; another was a rose with its outer
petals peeled back. The heads of other pins were fashioned
as various types of flowers, some with pearl settings. One
manufacturer in the early 1900's offered cards of six hatpins
terminating in female heads at a wholesale price of just $1.50
a card—and the tops were of sterling silver! Gold-plated pins
wholesaled at six on a card for as little as 75 cents.

Although early twentieth-century trade catalogues illus-
trate a few finger rings in the Art Nouveau manner, these
seem to be scarce in comparison with various other jewelry
items.

Those that are available are interesting not only because
of their design but also because of their mountings. Some
feature cameos cut in coral; others are set with diamonds,

amethysts, pearls, and opals. Less expensive ones have round, mirror-like gold fronts, and bands decorated with flowers and leaves.

Scarce, too, are charms, which were produced in near thousands of novelty shapes. On the other hand, a variety of Art Nouveau designs in sterling silver and gold-filled sleeve buttons are available, which should be of major interest to the button as well as the general Art Nouveau collector.

Barrettes, in widespread use years ago as clasps for holding women's hair, were made of various substances, including shell and our first commercial plastic, celluloid; and many of these were set with brilliants in a background of butterflies and intertwined flowers and vines. Solid gold barrettes measuring about 4 to 4½ inches long and 1 to 1⅞ inches high set with brilliants were wholesaling in 1914 for a mere 70 cents each; those of plastic, also set with brilliants, brought just 50 to 70 cents.

A revival of interest in Victorian jewelry began a few years ago, abetted by the publication of several books on the subject and by the spreading interest in small Victoriana generally. Contrary to popular belief, there were many fine Victorian jewelry craftsmen, even in the machine age. Now the interest in jewelry is extending beyond the Victorian period into the early twentieth century, and the focus is likely to be on Art Nouveau—even on those originally inexpensive commercial productions. Connoisseurs, of course, will scorn them, which leaves the field wide open to those collectors whose acquisitions must be paid for by leftover grocery and household money. In present-day America, beset at every turn by increasing taxes and galloping inflation, it is these collectors who are in the majority. Consequently, even without the connoisseurs the field will be crowded, and the prices are apt to rise as the demand presses sharply against the available supply.

The time to seek out these little items of jewelry is now.

Cultivate your neighborhood antique dealer (virtually all neighborhoods have dealers today), and let him know what you are looking for.

Watch the want ads in your home town newspaper for offerings of old jewelry, but try not to become the victim of a "setup." This is the "house" sale conducted by professionals who are not actually offering the contents of their homes for sale at all but are tendering merchandise they have specifically purchased to foist off on the unwary.

If you're interested in jewelry, study several of the good books available on the subject of gems. Talk with experts whenever you have the opportunity and visit museums that display jewelry. When you get to the point at which you can easily distinguish a genuine diamond from a zircon, you may be ready to go out and buy on your own. But until you get to that point, don't buy expensive jewelry unless the owner will permit you to take it to an expert for appraisal. You are likely to be charged a small fee, but this could save you loss of both pocketbook and face.

And remember that a good many individuals are forced to sell their personal heirlooms for such purposes as paying hospital or doctors' bills, taxes, and to meet other exigencies. Those who really know the value of what they are selling and who are offering their jewelry at bargain prices will usually permit you to obtain an appraisal if you will leave a deposit (or sometimes the full payment in the form of a postdated check) with them for security. After all, they may not know you either, and, for all they know, you could be a scoundrel (but of course you're not).

I know a school teacher who lives in a community near my own and who supplements her salary by buying and selling good early jewelry. She has studied the subject and she knows jewelry. She readily permits would-be purchasers to take items in which they are interested to an expert for an appraisal, and she will refund your money for any tentative purchase you make with which you are dissatisfied. This works out well both for her and her customers.

Some dealers who handle a general line of antiques occasionally carry some jewelry. Nearly always, but not invariably, they are familiar with the pieces they buy. In cases in which they are not, you may find a bargain—if you know jewelry and jewelry values yourself.

Increasing quantities of jewelry are being sold at the various antiques shows around the country. A lot is also cropping up at the outdoor flea markets, but the bulk of this is either junk or consists of cheap costume pieces. Sometimes, however, a bargain may be lurking even at a flea market.

V

Art Nouveau Silver

INTRIGUING PITCHER IN ART NOUVEAU STYLE MADE EARLY IN THIS CEN-
TURY. *The International Silver Company Historical Library.*

THROUGH THE YEARS, silver manufacturers have been prone to cling to tradition in designing tablewares. Early in the present century, the majority of these producers continued either to choose as their themes variations of rather chaste classic designs or to cherish the rococo—which had blossomed anew several times since its origination under Louis XV in the eighteenth century and which had been experiencing a field day in the final quarter of the nineteenth century. Some, however, fell under the mystical spell cast by Art Nouveau.

Notable among these in the United States were the Gorham Manufacturing Company of Providence, Rhode Island; Unger Brothers of Newark, New Jersey; R. Wallace & Sons Manufacturing Company of Wallingford, Connecticut; and Reed & Barton of Taunton, Massachusetts, together with several smaller firms.

Gorman produced the outstanding line of Art Nouveau silverware by a process known as Martelé work. The idea for this began to evolve in about 1895, and it was under the direction of William J. Codman, an imaginative and talented English silversmith, that the designs were developed. Each piece was unique, made entirely by hand, and had a silver content of 950/1000, which was above the 925/1000 required for sterling.

The Martelé pieces were wrought from flat sheets of silver entirely by the use of a hammer. Form was paramount, and the decoration reflected naturalistic forms—flowers, waves, mermaids, fish, cloud effects, and so on.

MARTELÉ TANKARD, CAPAC-
ITY 1½ PINTS, BY GORHAM.

DELIGHTFUL MARTELÉ
SILVER LAMP, 27 INCHES IN
HEIGHT OVERALL. *Courtesy,
The Gorham Company.*

MARTELÉ TANKARD WITH A
CAPACITY OF 8 PINTS. *Courtesy, The Gorham Com-
pany.*

MARTELÉ TANKARD WITH
CAPACITY OF 6½ PINTS.
*Courtesy, The Gorham
Company.*

There were a large number of failures at the outset, and no pieces were actually marketed until 1901 with production continuing for about a decade afterward.

Vases, bowls, and tankards were produced at first, then complete dinner services and numerous decorative and ornamental objects. An early memorandum in the files of the Gorham Company says that "the marks of the hammer are left apparent upon the surface, giving a soft, misty texture, which cannot be obtained in any other way."

Martelé was expensive by virtue of the taxing method of its creation and because of its high silver content. It was not unusual to color the surface of the metal when pieces were finished so that they showed various delicate metallic lusters. Sometimes the decoration stood out in bold relief as a leaf, tendril, or stem, and at other times it was almost lost in the surface of the metal until bolder relief was obtained by use of the craftsman's hammer.

The Jewelers' Circular-Weekly in its October 19, 1904, issue commented favorably upon a collection of Martelé pieces, singling out for special mention a centerpiece 35 inches long and 22½ inches high and a punch bowl, which it said was one of the finest pieces in the collection, adding: " 'Toilers of the Sea' is the title, and the figures in the water, the sunburst and the conquering human types, a female on the obverse and a male on the reverse, are all skilfully portrayed. The shape of the bowl lends itself admirably to the treatment of the mythological story told in the relief work."

The Martelé line ranged from candlesticks and tankards to tableware and cigar lighters and also included vases, large trophy cups, tall claret jugs, chocolate sets, and waiters. An interesting discussion of Martelé was presented by Katharine Morrison McClinton in the July, 1969, issue of *The Antiques Journal,* in which she pointed out that the company made no sets of flat silver in this ware but did produce individual table utensils.

Today, Martelé pieces have become choice collectors' items

PUNCH BOWL AND LADLE IN GORHAM'S MARTELÉ.
BOWL HAS A CAPACITY OF 16 PINTS. *Courtesy, The
Gorham Company.*

TWO MARTELÉ VASES BY GORHAM. THE ONE AT
LEFT IS 26 INCHES TALL AND THE ONE AT RIGHT IS
24½ INCHES. *Courtesy, The Gorham Company.*

with values on the rise. Mrs. McClinton also pointed out that a good many articles were made especially for such companies as Theodore B. Starr, of New York City, and Spaulding & Company, of Chicago. These were marked with the companies' individual names, plus the Martelé mark, which included Gorham's lion, an anchor and a G, atop which was an eagle with wings outspread. Sometimes, the word Martelé was also incorporated.

Gorham's Martelé pieces surrendered to both Art Nouveau form and decoration. Tall tankards and ewers with ripple-shaped handles looked pliant and ready to yield to the touch. Punch bowls and other bowls were designed with undulating rims that flowed in and out. So, too, were the rims of trays, decorated with vines and flowers, wheat sheaves, and fruit. Various adaptations of the whiplash line were patterned on such things as tea and coffee pots, kettles, and flatware. Sea creatures and insects were incorporated in designs on toilet set pieces.

Ladles were made with caputs featuring heads that appeared half-animal, half-human. There were candlesticks with whiplash handles ending in lily blossom shapes and with bell-like candle receptacles. One flower form candlestick was footed with the feet ending in paws and the knees shaped as heads. Cigar lighters in kettle shapes and chased with flower and vine designs had spouts terminating in flame points.

Scarcely less imaginative were the designers for Unger Brothers — jewelers, silversmiths, and glass cutters — who, shortly after the turn of this century, produced scores of Art Nouveau forms.

In 1906, when this firm had factory and salesrooms at 412–424 Halsey Street and 26–38 Beecher Street in Newark, it issued a folio-sized catalogue in which it introduced "the latest, most artistic, original and brilliant conceptions in Sterling Silverware." The company indicated it had discarded its old patterns and styles in favor of the new designs. A copy of this huge catalogue in the author's possession is filled with illustrations of silverwares made in the new style. Not all pieces were strictly Art Nouveau, but the majority were. This catalogue is invaluable for its life-size illustrations showing the American adaptation of Art Nouveau in dozens of silver pieces.

Sterling silver forks and spoons were produced in a pattern called La Fantasie, with handles in the form of a lithe female clad in a filmy garment. Her upstretched arms and flowing hair melted into and became a part of the caput, the top of which was adorned with a flower.

Similar, except that the woman was formed in profile, was a pattern named Les Secrete des Fleurs. Particularly Art Nouveau in form and decor was still another pattern, the Wave. In this, the upstretched hands of the maiden grasped at waves that formed the caput. Other new art patterns in sterling forks and knives were called Evangeline, Reine des Fleurs, Dawn, and Cupid Sunbeam. A food pusher was also made in the last-named patterns, as were baby knives, forks, and spoons.

Also Art Nouveau in its flower-and-vine decoration was Unger Brothers' Narcissus set, which included table knives and forks, a carving set, beef steak knife set, pie and butter knives, butter spreader, cheese scoop, butter pick, sardine, berry, olive, oyster, fish, and salad forks, cucumber server, ladles, and the following spoons: tea, soup, table, desert, five o'clock tea, coffee, bonbon, bouillon, sugar, mustard, olive, berry, preserve, and salad.

Other sterling silver articles manufactured by Unger Brothers in the Art Nouveau style included toilet sets, cigarette cases and match boxes, card and vanity cases, hand mirrors, military brushes, cloth brushes, whisk brooms, nail polishers, hairpin cases, nail files, button hooks, shoe horns, toothbrushes, paper cutters and creasers, scissors, picture frames, tea and coffee sets, berry bowls, bonbon and almond sets, bread trays, chocolate cups, mustard jars, tea strainers, candlesticks, pin trays, ashtrays, pincushions, card cases, lorgnettes, flasks, bottle openers, napkin rings, and novelties of numerous types.

Numerous miscellaneous silverwares showing a strong Art Nouveau influence were turned out early in this century by a group of relatively small, independent manufacturers, including Alvin Manufacturing Company of Newark, New Jersey, which made sterling silverware and novelties, plated wares, and silver deposit articles and whose name was changed to Alvin Corporation after its purchase in 1928 by the Gorham Corporation; Dominick & Haff of New York City and Newark, which was purchased by Reed & Barton in 1928; Homan Manufacturing Company of Cincinnati, Ohio, which produced electroplated wares; Daniel Low & Company of Salem, Massachusetts (it was Daniel Low who is generally given credit for originating the famous "Salem Witch" spoons); Mauser Manufacturing Company of Mt. Vernon, New York, which produced sterling novelties, hollowware, and cut glass with silver mounts (this company later merged with another as the Mt. Vernon Company Silversmiths and was subsequently acquired by Gorham); the Sterling Company of Providence, Rhode Island; F. M. Whiting & Company of North Attleboro, Massachusetts, which later became a division of Ellmore Silver Company but is now independently owned; Woodside Sterling Company of New York City; and E. G. Webster and Sons of North Attleboro, Massachusetts.

William B. Durgin Company of Concord, New Hampshire, widely known for its spoons, turned out interesting designs of Art Nouveau flatware. This company, founded literally on a shoestring by William B. Durgin, expanded substantially in the late nineteenth and the early twentieth centuries and also produced hollowware, novelties, and souvenir spoons. It was purchased by Gorham in 1905 and was moved to Providence, Rhode Island, at the beginning of the Depression in 1930.

Art Nouveau also influenced the silver-plate manufacturers, including William B. Rogers and a number of smaller companies in the United States, such as Theodore W. Foster & Brother Company, R. Blackinton & Company, and Paye & Baker. Most of the major designs had been discontinued before the end of the first decade of this century, although a number of plated wares and pieces with engraved or etched designs continued to be made for some years. Among these were numerous small novelty pieces such as match safes.

Many of the American silver manufacturers and producers of silver-plated goods issued pieces that were strictly Art Nouveau in character; others, however, incorporated certain Art Nouveau design elements—notably vines and flowers—in traditional shapes, so that these products became love children rather than legitimate offspring of the new style. The impact of the movement was particularly noticeable between 1900 and about 1910, after which point design deterioration set in, yielding articles that were flamboyant and tawdry.

Patterns in the Art Nouveau style or showing a strong influence produced by R. Wallace & Sons included those named Floral, Joan, and Blossom.

Wm. Rogers of Wallingford, Connecticut, produced patterns in the new style called Berwick, and Wm. A. Rogers produced patterns named Hanover, Sherwood, Carnation, Violet, Leyland, and Grenoble.

Wm. Rogers & Son patterns affected by the style included Arbutus and Flower.

Alvin Manufacturing Company produced several collectible patterns, among them Brides Bouquet, Majestic, Easter Lily, Raphael, and Fleur de Lis.

Rogers & Bro. produced the Mystic, Century, Berkshire, and Florette patterns.

Community Silver made a pattern called Flower-de-Luce and another termed Wildwood.

I have located only one Art Nouveau pattern made by The American Silver Company—Nenuphar—though it may also have made others.

Reed & Barton manufactured La Pariesenne, Les Cinq

Flowers, and Intaglio but also made numerous hollowware Art Nouveau design items with the pattern name of Modern Art and others assigned numbers, including style numbers 27, 32, 33, 35, 103, 105, 112, 220, 222, 240, 692, 1327, 1884, 4890, and 4933.

The above does not represent an all-inclusive list of patterns, but those listed may be watched for by collectors interested in assembling Art Nouveau sterling and plated silver. Such pieces crop up now and then in small antiques shops and even at flea markets.

The plated pieces of flatware have been seen in small shops and at flea markets priced at 25 cents to around $1 each, although special larger serving pieces are usually tagged a bit higher. Unless you have keen eyesight, it's advisable to carry a small magnifying glass, since many pieces are offered "as is" —that is, begrimed with dirt and dust, much of which will disappear when cleaned. Items that have had little wear can frequently be restored to their pristine beauty with the application of a good silver polish. There's little one can do, however, with pieces whose silver coat has worn off except to have them replated, which is a fairly costly process compared to original cost.

In England and Scotland, several multi-talented artists and artisans turned their attention to the design of some striking pieces of silver. Charles Robert Ashbee was one who, in addition to his remarkable pieces of silver jewelry plated with gold, designed a number of silverware articles. Ashbee was a follower of William Morris, and he founded the School and Guild of Handicraft in London. His own work in the Art Nouveau style was relatively restrained. Much of his silver was ornamented with semiprecious stones and enamels.

Fine silver designs were also achieved by Omar Ramsden and W. A. S. Benson, among others. English commercial producers of silver in the new style included the noted firm of Elkingtons, and W. Hutton & Sons.

In Glasgow, Scotland, some silverwares were made in the

new style by Margaret and Frances Macdonald, among others. The former, as noted earlier, became the wife of Charles Rennie Mackintosh, who also designed at least a few pieces of Art Nouveau silver.

A good bit of silver flatware produced about the turn of this century, while not fully Art Nouveau in character, did resemble the new style in spirit—notably in its motifs of intertwined flowers and flowing vines. There also were such articles as candlesticks and candelabra with convoluted bases and decorations of trailing vines, and Art Nouveau-inspired souvenir spoons, coffee pots, teapots and other tea wares, syrup jugs, butter dishes, and toast racks. Other individual silver table pieces included mustard pots, spoons, and sugar and cream sets.

Some striking silver flatware with emphasis on functional value was designed late in the movement by the Belgian Henri van de Velde, who, like so many prolific Art Nouveau designers and artisans, also created furniture, graphic designs, and adjuncts for interior decoration, although his primary training was as an architect. The silver was designed in Germany, where Van de Velde worked from about the beginning of this century. He also created such objects as candelabra and a tea service. Silver flatware was also designed by Richard Riemerschmid, of Munich, who began his career as a painter but who later reached out into other fields. The relatively few pieces designed by these and a few other outstanding figures in the Art Nouveau movement, however, are quite scarce and have largely been assimilated into museums and private collections. There is a striking silver jewel casket adorned with mother-of-pearl and turquoise enamel designed by Alexander Knox and executed by William Craythorne for Liberty of London now housed in the Museum of Modern Art in New York, which also has other pieces made for or by Liberty and Company. The Victoria and Albert Museum in London has a number of Art Nouveau creations in silver also designed for Liberty.

Other objects of Art Nouveau silver designed by Joseph Olbrich, Joseph Hoffman, Theodor Pogačnik, Albin Müller, Hugo Levin, Eric Ehrström, Torolf Pyrtz, and Thorvald Bindesbøll, among others, are preserved today in museums in Europe.

The influence of Art Nouveau permeated many of the productions of the M. S. Benedict Manufacturing Company of East Syracuse, New York, early in this century. This company produced in the new style silver- and gold-plated articles that included shelf or mantel clocks, paper cutters, candlesticks, match safes, blotters, inkstands, picture frames, hand mirrors, manicure accessories, and napkin rings.

Benedict made a candleholder with an undulating standard or shaft, from which two curved arms reached upward to support the candle receptacle. The base was shaped as a series of petals. These were turned out in French gray, Venetian bronze, and ormolu gold finishes at wholesale prices ranging from $18 to $24 a dozen.

A paper cutter was designed with an undulating shaft-handle and a three-petal top. The company made a match safe with a base shaped as a large leaf, and an inkstand with curved metal lines appearing to flow from the base to the top of the ink bottle receptacle.

Several types of Art Nouveau photograph frames were produced with waving metal stems extending from flowers at the top to the bottom of the frame. A novel production was a thermometer frame in heavy gold plate with asymmetrical elements forming two feet. These sold at wholesale, complete with thermometer, at $8 a dozen. Another intriguing article was a combination ashtray with asymmetrical borders and cigar cutter.

Benedict also made a delightful silver-plated napkin ring with a butterfly poised on top and with an asymmetrical base decorated with flowers and scroll-like vines, and another with a woodpecker perched on a stem with leaves on one side.

A considerable quantity of silver-deposit wares—articles

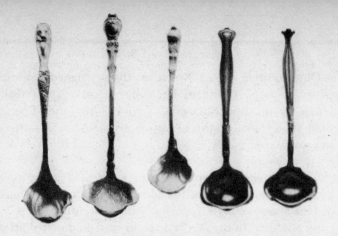

A GROUP OF GORHAM'S ART NOUVEAU PUNCH
LADLES IN ITS MARTELÉ LINE. *Courtesy, The Gorham Company.*

SOUVENIR SPOONS OF EARLY TWENTIETH CENTURY MADE OF
STERLING SILVER AND SHOWING THE ART NOUVEAU INFLU-
ENCE. THESE ORIGINALLY SOLD AT PRICES OF FROM ABOUT
$2.50 TO $4, BUT CURRENT VALUES ARE WELL ABOVE THESE.

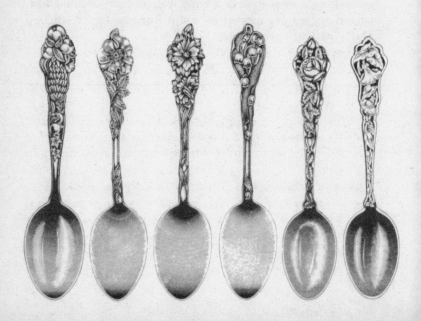

of glass with designs of sterling silver applied through electrolysis or other methods—was made in the Art Nouveau style from the opening of the century through the First World War. These included numerous types of vases, jugs, pitchers, plates, tumblers, bottles, and other utilitarian and decorative pieces.

Silver-deposit wares had also been made in some quantity in the 1880's and 1890's, and undoubtedly even earlier, and electricity was used in addition to deposit designs of gold, copper, and other metals on glass objects. Several methods patented last century for depositing metals on glass are described by Albert Christian Revi in his *Nineteenth Century Glass: Its Genesis and Development,* and readers who are interested in the technical processes are referred to that excellent book.

The Art Nouveau decor on the twentieth-century pieces was primarily floral in character and featured flowers with extremely long and flowing stems and vines. Such pieces were made by most of the silver manufacturers mentioned earlier in this chapter. Some intriguing pieces in this style were offered in 1914 at the following wholesale prices: 10-inch-tall vase, $6.05; 54-ounce capacity jug, $4.05, or the same jug with six matching tumblers, $8.13; quart bottle, $6.75; 9-inch diameter sandwich plate, $2.70, and $10\frac{1}{2}$-inch plate, $3.35; vinegar bottle, $2.45 and $3.35; finger bowl, $1.65; 8-inch-tall candlestick, $2.70; salt and pepper shakers, $2.70 a pair; handled nappies, 5 inches in diameter, $2.95; sherbet glass, 69 cents; and olive dish, 90 cents.

Literally scores of miscellaneous objects, including novelties, were fashioned in the commercial Art Nouveau style from early in this century until the late 1920's in both sterling and plated silver. Available for collectors at prices far from exorbitant are numerous souvenir spoons, although there already are numerous collectors in this field.

Of course, thousands of souvenir spoons were produced to commemorate persons, places, and events, but a large group made by numerous manufacturers also appeared in floral designs smacking strongly of Art Nouveau. Pages of jewelry wholesalers' and manufacturers' catalogues issued between 1905 and 1914 are filled with them. Flowers, often stylized, and vines adorn the caput and handles and sometimes flow over into the top edge of the bowls. In addition, such decorations also grace numerous after-dinner coffee and tea spoons. Quantities of these were offered in sterling silver in the 1912 catalogue of Albert Brothers, wholesale jewelers, of Cincinnati, Ohio, at prices ranging from $1 to $2 each, and the souvenir spoons in sterling were available for from $1.50 to $1.80.

Birth or month spoons, once popular as gifts, were manufactured in the Art Nouveau style. These were offered in sterling in the 1910 catalogue of Wallenstein, Mayer & Company, wholesale jewelers also of Cincinnati, at $1.50 each. The same company tendered souvenir spoons at $1.50 to $3 in sterling.

In addition to floral souvenir spoons, Otto Young & Company of Chicago, which claimed to be the largest wholesale jewelry house in the world, presented in its 1907 catalogue one spoon whose handle was partly formed by a lithe, bare-bosomed female with one hand aloft, clasping a seashell in the caput. It was designated the Mermaid pattern. Otto Young also offered the floral decor souvenir spoons with raised blossoms, leaves, and vines mounted on cards containing six sterling spoons and wholesaling for only $5.65 a card. Similar cards containing six sterling floral coffee spoons were available at only $3.75 a card. In its 1915 catalogue, this company advertised Art Nouveau souvenir spoons on cards of six each at $8 a card, and the coffee spoons had advanced to $4.70 a card. Also available were Art Nouveau baby spoons with what were advertised as "crooked handles."

For the souvenir spoon collector, several good books available are listed in the Selected Bibliography. Perhaps the most exhaustive study is included in *American Spoons* by Dorothy

T. Rainwater and Donna H. Felger, a profusely illustrated book published in late 1969 by Thomas Nelson & Sons and Everybodys Press.

The Forbes Silver Company, which became a part of International Silver Company of Meriden, was giving some emphasis to the new art in 1911 and 1912 in a variety of miscellaneous silver-plated articles, including crumb sets, napkin rings, toilet wares, brushes, and jewel boxes.

Several companies specialized in Art Nouveau napkin rings of plated silver, the majority featuring undulating rims and bands of flowers with long stems around the exterior. Fairly heavy sterling napkin rings were also made in similar style and wholesaled at prices of $2 to $3.50 each more than half a century ago.

It was in silver- and gold-plated jewelry boxes, however, that the Art Nouveau designers had a field day. These were being presented by the score between the first of this century and 1930 in numerous shapes, sizes, and designs. Many were footed. Some had small fancy handles. Nearly all were lined with colored silk or satins. All types of flowers and vines were employed in the embossed decoration that virtually covered the entire exterior of many such boxes. Some had hinged lids or covers, and others had tops that simply lifted off.

A small one, measuring just 4 x 3 x 2½ inches, was offered in Otto Young's 1915 catalogue at a wholesale price of $1.25 silver-plated or $1.50 gold-plated. Larger boxes wholesaled for from $3 to $6.50. Some were offered as either jewel or handkerchief boxes. The less expensive ones were usually plated white metal. The boxes are currently being reproduced and the reproductions cost nearly the same as the originals—from $7.50 to about $15. They may be found in gift shops and related establishments but some are likely, sooner or later, to find their way into the hands of a few antiques dealers. Given some minor signs of wear, they will be difficult to distinguish from the earlier boxes.

Various other types of boxes or containers are available in Art Nouveau styles in both sterling and plated silver. Simpson, Hall, Miller & Company of Wallingford, Connecticut, which had brought out an Art Nouveau flatware pattern called Berwick, presented in one of its catalogues early in this century an intriguing embossed silver playing-card case with Art Nouveau decor.

Art Nouveau definitely invaded the sterling and plated match box or match safe field, and although apparently many of these containers were manufactured and sold, they seem to be fairly scarce today. A good many were decorated with supple maidens sans clothing in languid poses.

Other types of small boxes or containers strongly influenced by the new designs included stamp boxes, court plaster cases, and salve jars. The sterling and silver-plated tops of many puff jars also were of the new art design, as were those of hair receivers. Puff jars and hair receivers were made of cut glass, pressed glass, porcelain, and metals.

Other silver and plated articles to watch out for in this field are hand mirrors, combs and brushes, various manicure accessories from buffers to nail clippers, small scissors, curling irons, cheese dishes, tea caddies, tureens, covered vegetable dishes, waiters and other trays, mugs and cups, nut bowls, jewel trees, paper and envelope racks, pen trays and miscellaneous dresser trays, cane and umbrella heads, mesh purses, bread trays, picture frames (several were advertised in 1918 as being Art Nouveau in pattern), shaving sets, knives, cigarette cases, book marks, letter openers, pencil cases, hatpin holders, hatpins themselves, bag checks, fern dishes, and—of all delightful things—eyeglass holders.

Some of these articles will be discussed in greater detail in subsequent chapters.

VI

Clocks, Watches, and Their Accessories

ART NOUVEAU INFLUENCED WATCHCASE MAKERS TO SOME EXTENT. THESE WATCHES WERE ALL MADE SHORTLY AFTER THE TURN OF THIS CENTURY. THOSE IN THE TOP ROW ARE SIZE 16, AND THE TWO AT LEFT WERE MADE BY CRESCENT. THE CASES ARE GOLD. THOSE BELOW ARE SIZE 0 AND ARE GOLD. THE TWO AT LEFT WERE MADE BY WALTHAM AND THE ONE AT FAR RIGHT BY CRESCENT. THE ONE SECOND FROM LEFT AT BOTTOM IS SET WITH DIAMONDS.

WHILE THE MORE SERIOUS STUDENT of the art of horology might spurn them, quite a large number of clocks and watches were produced in the Art Nouveau vein. Some of them, it's true, border on the atrocious, but others are quite charming and still others are at least intriguing. There seem to be some collectors today who specialize in what has been rather broadly termed "conversation pieces." A good many of the clocks in the new style will definitely fall into that category.

At least a few Art Nouveau designs were turned out by most of the major clock manufacturers in the United States. Their cases were primarily of porcelain and metals, though some were of wood. A large percentage of the porcelain-case clocks were made by the Ansonia and Gilbert factories, which ran them off on a mass production basis. More than a few of these actually represented a crossbreed in which the rococo was mated to Art Nouveau. Royal Bonn, however, did construct several porcelain cases that were in full character with the new style, with emphasis on asymmetry in shape and with naturalistic decor. Among these were clocks given the names La France, La Floride, Le Fleur, Le Friese, La Paline, La Fontaine, La Chartres, and La Mine. These were all being offered in 1910 at wholesale prices ranging from $9 to $18. These cases were fitted with eight-day movements and were enameled in tints and shades of green, blue, and red. Some came with French and others with American sash and dials. The clocks measured from $9\frac{1}{4}$ to $14\frac{1}{2}$ inches in height and from $9\frac{1}{2}$ to $12\frac{1}{2}$ inches in width. They were advertised as "decorated in New Arts."

Cast metal clock in the commercial Art Nouveau style, 1907. Made by Western Clock Company with a 32-hour movement.

Commercial Art Nouveau Ansonia clock, the "tulip"; first decade of twentieth century. This had a one-day movement and was given a gold finish.

Intriguing group of novelty Art Nouveau clocks. Clock at left in top row is trademarked "J B., Ormulu": the one in the center is gold-plated and made by New Haven Clock Company; and the one at right is an Ansonia bronze clock. The two at right in the bottom row are New Haven and the one at the extreme left is an Ansonia "Florentine." These all were offered in the first decade of this century.

Some of the Ansonia porcelain-case clocks were enhanced by Wedgwood-cameo-type decorations of flowers, maidens, and cupids. These were named Cameo, and each type was assigned a number. Other Ansonia Art Nouveau clock names included Armor, Agate, Anchor, Gazelle, Glory, La Clairmont, La Chapelle, La Platta, La Chartres, Triad, La Layon, and La Cruz. Some of the cases for the Ansonia clocks were made of Royal Bonn porcelain.

Gilbert's porcelain clocks in this style bore identification numbers, and the colors in which these were decorated included cobalt blue, ruby, pink, green, and violet.

The great majority of Art Nouveau clocks, however, were made of metal, many of them plated with either silver or gold. Judging by the frequency of their appearance in manufacturers' catalogues during the first quarter of this century, they were extremely popular and for the most part—since they were all mass produced—were quite cheap, wholesale prices starting at around $2. Ansonia made a number of them in bronze. Other producers included New Haven Clock Company, Jennings Bros. Manufacturing Company, Western Clock Company, New Haven Clock Company, Gilbert Clock Company, Waterbury Clock Company, Seth Thomas, and some of the smaller companies.

The less expensive metal clocks were equipped with cheap one-day movements, but better ones ran for eight days on a full winding.

The Seth Thomas line included a variety of asymmetrical cases with cast flowers and leaves and occasionally the head of a maiden with flowing locks. The cases were given an ormolu finish to imitate the appearance of gold. (Ormolu is an alloy of copper and zinc.) The better clocks were equipped with a cathedral bell movement and wholesaled in 1907 at close to $20.

Ansonia produced a gold-plated metal clock with whiplash lines forming the case's outlines and with a cast figure of a woman strumming a mandolin on the base. It was called

Harmony. Waterbury fashioned one with a case formed largely of flowing, intertwined lines with a poppy on top and a cupid figure playing a lute on one side. It was called Petard and wholesaled for $5.50.

Winged cupid figures to supplement the floral and flowing decor of these clocks were popular, and they were utilized in almost every conceivable pose—holding the clock, hugging one another, reading, aiming arrows, ...

Female heads with flowing hair were also popular, their position normally being assigned to the lower half of the clocks. Most boasted a flower in their locks, and a few figures included torsos with bare breasts. Western made one clock with a full-length figure clothed in a diaphanous garment that flowed to the base of the case. Gilbert also made one with a seated full-length figure surrounded by flowing vines that provided the skeleton of the bottom half of the case. Western's Nymph, of ormolu-plated cast metal, featured a winged cupid embracing a nymph in a flowing garment that formed a part of the clock's base.

Manufactured also in metal were clock sets that consisted of a clock and either two vases or a pair of candelabra. Seth Thomas made a set with two vases in 1910 in what it characterized as "Art Nouveau finish." The clock had a fifteen-day movement, stood on a base with curving legs, and the lower half was decorated with the head of a woman observing a butterfly. This was called the Dorothy set, and the clock could be purchased separately for $34 wholesale or together with the vases, each decorated with a winged cupid's head, for $45.

Waterbury issued a line of gilt metal clocks with celluloid dials that wholesaled for $2.25 to $2.75 in 1910, and similar ones with ivory dials at prices of $4.75 to $5.35.

So many varieties of these inexpensive Art Nouveau clocks came off the assembly lines early in the twentieth century that one could easily fill an entire house with them without duplication.

WATCH FOB, GOLD-FILLED WITH SIGNET SEAL ON BOTTOM. CA. 1907.

FANTASTICALLY AMUSING BUTTERFLY CLOCK OF BRASS WITH GOLD GILT AND INLAID WITH GLASS. CLOCK, ALARMED, OPERATED A DAY ON ONE WINDING AND DATES ABOUT 1905.

Inexpensive alarm clocks were also created in the Art Nouveau style, as were traveling clocks with both metal and leatherette cases. A rather fantastic imported alarm was made of brass in the shape of a butterfly. The butterfly had glass eyes. This little monstrosity wholesaled for $6.70 in 1905. Some alarm clocks had cases fashioned of metal vines or ribbons with their mercurial ends tied in bow knots at top and base. Probably because they were so frequently discarded when they were broken or their mechanisms got out of order, these alarm clocks appear to be quite scarce today.

Vast numbers of wooden mantel clocks, made chiefly in oak, featured floral decor and curving lines. Principally, however, these were of the rococo type, although some showed a leaning toward the new art. Clocks of this type originally sold for only a few dollars but are now bringing $65 and up in the antiques shops.

Almost no hanging wall clocks seem to have been made in the Art Nouveau style, nor were there many of the so-called marbleized clocks with their metal columns and, often, cast bronze tablets.

As for watches in general, the Art Nouveau influence is seen almost altogether in case decoration rather than shape. However, Waltham made some ladies' watches with the ring tops designed in what the company termed Art Nouveau Bows.

Usually, however, the new art's influence resulted in floral case decorations that featured lilies and other long-stemmed flowers, some stylized, occasionally with the added attraction of a small bird. Sometimes the flowers framed a miniature scene or house. Some blossoms seemed to be thrust upward by their sinuous stems. Quite a number of Crescent pocket watches for men, manufactured by the Crescent Watch Case Company, were made with floral Art Nouveau decorations that were striking in their sinuosity.

The New England Watch Company produced for the 1907 trade a line of gold-filled and sterling silver watches that were definitely Art Nouveau, featuring both flowers and feminine heads.

Most of the major watch manufacturers turned out some of these new art designs, but in most of them little creative imagination is evidenced.

Right now, however, many collectors are devoting major attention to gold and gold-filled watches, and the chatelaine women's watches are becoming increasingly popular, so that antique dealers are stocking watches in ever larger numbers. This provides the Art Nouveau collector with an opportunity to look over larger stocks of watches than has been the case in the past. Along with various articles of silver, gold watches are considered excellent investments and are looked upon by many as providing a better hedge against inflation than money in a savings account.

Also produced in Art Nouveau styles were some watch guard and neck chains, vest chains, and fobs. The chains were made in solid gold, of gold plate, or were gold-filled and came in a diversity of sizes and designs. The art was evidenced in the slides of the chains, some of which were in the shape of blossoms enclosing a feminine head. Slides of the finer chains were often set with pearls, opals, or other stones. In vest chains, these slides frequently had gold fronts with floral engraving. Some came complete with charms in the Art Nouveau style. There were leather vest chains with Art Nouveau slides, featuring flowers or variations of the whiplash line.

There were seals on fob chains of silk and other materials that were strictly commercial Art Nouveau, including, naturally, that favorite, the woman's head with flowing hair. The fob vest chains also were made of gold-filled metal and gold-filled woven wire.

Neck chains for the ladies occasionally featured Art Nouveau decor in the small charms attached by a ring to the chain's extremity.

Of special interest to the collector in this area was a gold-filled fob chain that consisted of a series of five feminine heads, the long locks of each forming whiplash curves, the last ending in a signet seal. Another consisted of three female heads, their long locks flowing around their necks. This was offered in a rose-colored finish. One black silk safety fob bore a seal formed of three trumpet-form flowers with intertwined stems. These were made of 14-karat gold, and this fob wholesaled in 1907 for $4.25. It measured six inches in length.

Ladies' chatelaine chains, too, were produced with brooch attachments of women's heads, some were set with fancy stones.

Watch charms—solid gold, gold-filled, or of rolled gold plate—were available separately in a wide price range, and a number of these boasted decorations in the new art style. Some of these were also set with various types of stones, the less expensive ones having imitation opals and rubies, blood-stones, carnelians, or goldstones. Crosses, of course, were extremely popular as watch or other charms, and a small percentage of these were manufactured in the Art Nouveau tradition and were made of gold, silver, and plated metal.

Good places to look for Art Nouveau watches and accessories are antiques shows, most of which attract one or more dealers who specialize in jewelry and kindred articles. Antique jewelry specialists also advertise in the various collector periodicals. Some will send you photographs for a small deposit, which is usually refunded either when a purchase is made or the photograph is returned. There are a few of these specialists who advertise that they will send small assortments of goods to "responsible persons" on approval.

VII

Of Special Feminine Interest

Intriguing silver pin trays such as this one by Unger Brothers reflects the extension of Art Nouveau into milady's boudoir.

THERE ARE CERTAINLY specific categories of collectible items that hold more interest for women than for men—and vice versa. Among the small collectible objects that have, or should have, a particular appeal for the ladies are combs and barrettes, manicure sets or accessories, toilet sets, chatelaine purses, brushes of various kinds, hand mirrors, and other articles that once graced milady's dressing table or were hidden away somewhere in her boudoir.

Many of these small objects were affected by the vogue for Art Nouveau, but apparently little or nothing has been written about them to date. Few of them, too, are yet in museums or the large private collections of better publicized and costlier objects of this short-lived period. Yet they constitute interesting, if not tremendously valuable, manifestations of the new art of the late nineteenth and early twentieth centuries and should, for that reason if for no other, be preserved.

Although interest in Art Nouveau during the years it flourished was not as widespread or as intense in the United States as it was in England and certain countries on the Continent, it did have some impact on designers and manufacturers in a variety of fields. Except for glass and a small amount of architecture, Art Nouveau attracted relatively few individuals in this country who were endowed with high artistic talents. But its vogue induced lesser talents to set their imaginations and their hands to work. The result was a variety, if not a flood, of merchandise revealing the movement's influence, even though its quality was a far cry from that of the furniture, jewelry, posters, and the adjuncts of interior decoration conceived by the gifted artists and artisans of other areas.

In those earlier years when our grandmothers and great-grandmothers let their shimmering locks grow, sometimes to great length, side and back combs for the hair were essential. Late last century, tortoise shell, long a favorite for combs, was largely replaced by celluloid. This was grained and colored to imitate tortoise shell and was considerably cheaper. Numerous celluloid combs of this type showed the impact of Art Nouveau upon their designers.

Particularly the decoration of the comb tops, large quantities of which bore the familiar flowers with long tendrils or stems, was characteristic of so much Art Nouveau design. Lilies with flowing stems linked to one another provided one design. Leaf designs adorned another. A peacock with wings outspread graced the top of one back comb. Still another featured a parade of sea creatures. A barrette was decorated with butterflies and flowers.

Many of these combs and barrettes had gold mountings to form the designs and some were set with brilliants, baroque pearls, topazes, sapphires, emeralds, amethysts, and other stones.

A 1914 catalogue of the A. C. Becken Company of Chicago offered a diversity of back and side combs and barrettes in a wholesale price range of from 55 cents to $7 each. A set of a back comb and two side combs with inlaid gold Art Nouveau designs of flowers and leaves and set with amethysts and brilliants was offered at $4.

Art Nouveau designs also characterized some imitation shell hair braid pins, a few of which appeared in curvilinear outline shape. Many were set with stones with designs inlaid in gold.

Since the commercial plastic celluloid is now "antique" in its own right, having first been devised in this country more than a century ago, numerous objects made in whole or in

CLOTH BRUSH (TOP), HAIR-
BRUSH, AND LADIES' CELLULOID
COMB, ALL WITH STERLING
SILVER TOPS OR TRIMMINGS,
DATE EARLY IN THIS CENTURY.

ART NOUVEAU HAND MIRROR
WITH STERLING BACK AND
FRENCH BEVELED PLATE MIR-
ROR GLASS, 1907.

STERLING SILVER BACKS OR TOPS
WITH ART NOUVEAU DECOR GRACE
THIS SET OF EARLY TWENTIETH-CEN-
TURY TOILET WARE, WHICH INCLUDES
HAIRBRUSH, BEVELED PLATE MIRROR,
CLOTH BRUSH, AND COMB. ORIGINAL
WHOLESALE PRICES OF THESE ARTI-
CLES WERE, FROM LEFT, $4.84,
$11.75, $4, AND $1.75.

part of celluloid—almost always grained and colored to imitate shell—are beginning to attract a following. Some antiques shops report they have customers on a waiting list for these celluloid collectibles. Right now prices are low for such things as combs, brushes, and manicure accessories, but they are likely to escalate as the demand for the earlier pieces increases.

Hatpins and hatpin holders did not escape the Art Nouveau vogue. Numerous hatpins of solid gold, rolled gold, sterling silver, or gold-fill bore hand-engraved designs of the familiar flowers and leaves; others had tops made of sinuous coils of metal. A good many tops were set with precious or semiprecious stones, including pearls, amethysts, aquamarines, sapphires, topazes, and rubies. There were hatpins with butterfly tops, and some in sterling silver had tops in the shape of women's heads, almost invariably with flowing hair.

Hatpin holders were made of both porcelain and metal, including sterling silver. The latter were used interchangeably as either hatpin or violet holders. Some stood on bases; others had ribbons by which they could be hung. A number were turned out in Art Nouveau designs of convoluted lines and stylized flowers.

Unger Brothers, certainly near the top among producers of Art Nouveau silver, created a truly fascinating variety of sterling hatpin holders; they were characteristic of the style in both form and decoration. Some stood on round bases, but others were equipped with hooks decorated with fancy ribbons. Some were actually in the form of attenuated flowers. Some had petal tops. Any of them would prove a choice collector's item today.

A great profusion of Art Nouveau toilet articles, such as combs, brushes, and hand mirrors, were created by the silver and silverplating companies. Because so many were produced, they are still relatively plentiful and should have a particular appeal to women.

Here, again, Unger Brothers was a leader in the field. Its

EARLY TWENTIETH-CENTURY ART NOUVEAU HAND MIRROR IN UNGER BROTHERS' "REINE DES FLEURS" (QUEEN OF FLOWERS) PATTERN.

STRIKING EXAMPLE OF THE ART NOUVEAU STYLE IN A STERLING SILVER MIRROR MADE BY UNGER BROTHERS IN 1906. THIS IS THE COMPANY'S "LE SECRÈTE DES FLEURS" DESIGN.

toilet sets included, in addition to the above-named pieces, various sizes of clothes brushes, manicure accessories, jars for vaseline, puffs, soap, tooth powder and talcum powder, hairpin and hairbrush bottles, toothbrushes, curlers, button hooks, glove stretchers, jewel cases, and combs for the gentlemen. All of these are highly collectible and were created in numerous shapes and designs.

Unger's Art Nouveau toilet sets were made under the following pattern names: May Blossom, Christmas Rose, Oriental Poppy, Gladiolus, Queen Rose, Maiden Hair Fern, Intaglio, Springtime, Reine des Fleurs, He Loves Me, Les Secrete des Fleurs, Evangeline, Love's Dream, and Lily.

A supple woman in a flowing garment formed the handle of the comb in the Les Secrete des Fleurs pattern. In the Reine des Fleurs pattern the handle was the sheathed lower limbs of a woman, whose upper torso was embossed on the comb's back. Hand mirrors of these patterns were made in matching forms. Clothes brushes in the same two patterns were created with undulating outlines, as were those in the Queen Rose, Evangeline, and Lily patterns.

Outlines of hat brushes were either curved or rectangular in shape, their tops embossed with writhing designs. Bonnet brushes in the patterns named above ranged from 6¾ to a little more than 7½ inches in height and were from 4 to 5½ inches in width across the bristles.

Tops and handles of the nail polishers were little short of fabulous, and some patterns came in two sizes. Pocket combs were housed in Art Nouveau silver cases, and some of these small combs were hinged to their cases.

Manicure accessories included nail files, nail buffs, pairs of curved and straight scissors, tweezers, and cuticle and corn knives. Handles of all these were produced in the patterns listed. So were the handles of toothbrushes, shoe horns, and button hooks, and the sterling tops of two sizes of puff jars and of the glass tooth and talcum powder holders.

Baby hairbrushes and combs were also made in the Art

CLOTHES BRUSH WITH STER-
LING SILVER HANDLE IN UNGER
BROTHERS' "REINE DES
FLEURS" PATTERN.

AN APPEALING THER-
MOMETER HOUSED IN A
SILVER CASE DESIGNED
BY UNGER BROTHERS.

NAIL POLISHER WITH IN-
TENSELY UNDULATING HANDLE.
THE PATTERN IS UNGER
BROTHERS' "LE SECRÈTE DES
FLEURS."

ART NOUVEAU PINCUSHION IN
SILVER BASE BY UNGER BROTH-
ERS, CA. 1906–7.

SILVER LORGNETTES AF-
FECTED THE NEW STYLE
EARLY IN THIS CENTURY,
AS WITNESS THIS UNGER
BROTHERS EXAMPLE.

BABY'S HAIRBRUSH BY
UNGER BROTHERS WITH
THE SENTIMENTAL PAT-
TERN NAME OF "THE
STOLEN KISS." BACK OF
THIS BRUSH IS STERLING
SILVER.

MEMO TABLETS SUCH AS
THIS ONE IN STERLING SIL-
VER BY UNGER BROTHERS
WERE ATTACHED TO A
LADY'S PERSON, SOMETIMES
AS PART OF A CHATELAINE,
TO REMIND HER OF CHORES
TO BE DONE.

STERLING SILVER JEWEL
CASE BY UNGER BROTHERS
LINED WITH VELVET HAD
HINGED COVER.

Nouveau patterns, and powder puffs were attached to sterling handles in these patterns.

Even though the art of sewing may soon vanish into the mists of time insofar as the average homemaker is concerned, pincushions can be charming objects to collect. A few of these showed the influence of the new style. Unger Brothers made one in flower form and others with velvet or plush cushions housed in sterling-decorated round cases.

In addition to its line of paper cutters (or letter openers), Unger also manufactured sterling silver paper creasers, whose handles were Art Nouveau.

Sterling card cases with chased Art Nouveau designs were made in two types—with hinged sides, and with pull-off tops. The former were carried by silver chains. Leather card cases were manufactured by many leather goods houses with small sterling silver shields in the Art Nouveau style.

The fashion for the lorgnette has diminished, but some years ago no millionaire's lady who wanted to evidence *bon ton* would have been caught at the opera or the corner saloon without a pair of those elegant eyeglasses mounted on a long handle. It will come as news to many collectors, but early in this century the Art Nouveau lorgnette was *the* thing.

There were really delightful lorgnette handles with chased and embossed decorations of demure maidens, roses and other flowers, leaves, and buds with whiplash stems. Unger Brothers crafted some intriguing ones in sterling. Also manufactured in this style were eyeglass holders with automatic reels and chains by which they could be fastened to the person, preventing many a lady from losing her eyeglasses. There were holders of gold, silver, and enamel, as well as gold-filled and gold-plated ones. These are scarce today but their pursuit can be great fun, and they are so small that even a large collection will require only a small space for display.

Baby rattles of one sort or another have been utilized almost since time immemorial to induce babies to forget their woes and quiet their screams, and one would hardly suspect

EVEN AUTOMATIC EYEGLASS HOLDERS DID NOT ESCAPE THE ART NOUVEAU INFLUENCE. THESE COULD BE HAD EITHER SILVER-PLATED OR GOLD-FILLED IN 1905.

GOLD-FILLED EYEGLASS CHAINS OF 1905 WITH HAIRPINS ATTACHED. THE ORNAMENTS WERE ENAMELED.

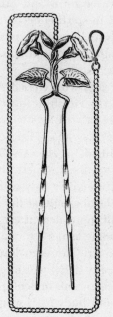
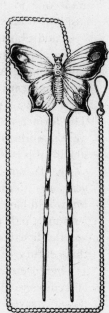

CURLING IRON IN THE 1905 MANNER WITH STERLING SILVER HANDLE ORIGINALLY WHOLESALED FOR $11.

that Art Nouveau would have invaded this rather remote area. Yet it did. A sterling rattle was made that depicts on its nether extremity (that's the extremity opposite the handle) a winged cupid planting a kiss smack on the lips of a bare-breasted lady. One will get you ten that these were purchased by fathers, not mothers, for their obstreperous offspring. Other rattles were embossed with flowers with long tendrils, and even those with jesters were accorded Art Nouveau treatment.

While we are not positive that the day of the lady's oval garter with fancy bow (the kind saloon girls love to display in western movies) is completely passé, these, too, were accorded the Art Nouveau treatment, though it was confined to their small buckles, often in sterling silver. New style designs made by Unger bore such names as Carnation, Violet, Lily, Lily of the Valley, Rose, Daisy, Water Lily, Poppy, Cosmos, Chrysanthemum, and Holly, and they were termed floral birthday garters.

Various other establishments also made similar garters of silk elastic webbing with the Art Nouveau shields of sterling. The highest wholesale price asked per pair of these by Otto Young in 1907 was $3.75 and the lowest was $1.75. (Quite similar shields were mounted on men's suspenders and on women's side elastic garters.)

Perhaps the best place to search for these early garters is among your grandmothers' effects, long stored away in basement or attic. The elastic webbing may have deteriorated, but an application of silver polish may well be able to restore the sparkling effect of the sterling shield.

Delightful collectible objects are the very small pocket mirrors, some of which also contained a powder puff. These were made of both sterling and plated silver and were of two general types—handled and oval. The latter had tiny rings by which they could be attached to chatelaines or elsewhere on the person. Those with handles averaged about 4½ inches in length, and the oval ones were 2 inches or less in diameter. Similar were the tiny oval chatelaine puff boxes and also a

group of bonbon boxes, which usually contained mints, ca-
chous, or what the English call "comfits" to freshen the breath.
Comfits included such things as caraway seeds, cloves, and
other herbs. The French called these little boxes *bonbon-
ières*. Bonbon boxes were made of metal, usually silver, or
enamels. Bonbon scoops, too, were produced in Art Nouveau
forms and designs. There was one in the shape of an open-
petaled flower with a twisted ring handle. The scoops obvi-
ated the need to pick up bonbons with the fingers from the
larger bonbon dishes and trays that graced many a turn-of-the
century home.

In a similar category, but larger than the pocket mirrors
and chatelaine puff boxes, were face powder "books," thin,
rectangular boxes, usually of sterling, and intended to hold
just what their name indicates. Early twentieth-century vanity
cases of sterling or plated silver sometimes bore Art Nouveau
designs.

Other small Art Nouveau collectibles that should have a
direct appeal for the ladies include tape measures, hem
gauges, needle cases, thimble cases, and memo tablets.

VIII

Of Special Interest to Men

MANY A SMOKER'S DEN EARLY IN THIS CENTURY WAS BRIGHTENED WITH SILVER ASHTRAYS FEATURING LISSOME LADIES IN FLOWING DIAPHANOUS RAIMENT. *Unger Brothers.*

THERE HAVE LONG been groups of collectible objects that have held a particular appeal for the male of the species. These include pipes, pocket knives, match boxes, or safes, flasks, and other commodities that—at least until recent years —have had a more intimate association with male than female.

In addition to these rather traditional collectibles, there are now available for the gentlemen a diversity of what may one day become artifacts of a bewildered era and which even now are mature enough to be plucked by those with an eye for antiques of the future. Those that we will discuss in this chapter were produced in or were influenced by the Art Nouveau movement and were made in relatively limited quantities.

Adjuncts of smoking (a habit now being roundly belabored) have perhaps become almost as much associated in the past few years with women as with men, although as yet male smokers of pipes and cigars seem to predominate. Cigar jars, therefore, should be of prime interest to men.

These containers have been made for a good many years in glass, wood, ceramics, and metal, but a small group associated with Art Nouveau primarily through their metal tops were produced between about 1910 and 1918. They were chiefly of glass with round silver or silver-plated tops, decorated with embossed floral or geometrical designs, either directly in the mode of or strongly imitative of the Art Nouveau style.

CIGARETTE CASE IN
STERLING BY UNGER
BROTHERS.

SILVER MATCH SAFE IN-
CORPORATES THE COMMER-
CIAL ART NOUVEAU ELE-
MENTS. IT WAS OFFERED BY
UNGER BROTHERS IN 1906.

CIGAR BOX IN GORHAM'S MARTELÉ MEASURES 12⅜ INCHES IN LENGTH.
Courtesy, The Gorham Company.

These jars were mostly made of crystal, some of it etched and pressed in molds, that imparted several basic pattern shapes. Octagonal glass containers appeared to have been most popular. Some were made with loops and thumbprint designs in the glass. Star designs were often impressed in the bases.

The containers ranged from about 5¾ to 7 inches in height and averaged from 3¾ to 5 inches in diameter. Some of the tops were made of so-called German silver—a white alloy of copper, zinc, and nickel. Many were fitted with a sponge and sponge holder to keep the cigars moist and prevent them from drying out. Some tops were silver-plated; others were gold-plated. The containers actually were used to hold both tobacco and cigars, and some were advertised as "cigar and tobacco" jars.

Their original prices during the period of World War I were from about $1.50 to around $6 for those with plated tops. Those with silver tops were scarcer and higher in price. Some of the tops were flat or slightly raised in the center and some had knobs by which they could be lifted off the glass containers.

Ashtrays were far more abundantly manufactured in the new art style. Unger Brothers turned out a variety of them in silver. Some were quite small, measuring only 3 inches in diameter, but some as large as 8 inches in diameter also were produced. Unger made a lovely ashtray, the center of which was a languid silver woman. Her flowing tresses and filmy robe formed the asymmetrical rim. An appealing young female nude appeared in the top of the base of another Unger creation, whose design resembled a seashell. Still another, in the commercial style, featured an embossed woman with long hair smoking a cigarette. Another had a lovely female head and torso surrounded by daisies and whiplash lines.

One novel silver ashtray was made in the shape of the man-in-the-moon smoking a pipe with the head of a woman on one side and her locks flowing around on the other.

MATCH SAFES OF STERLING SILVER IN THE ART NOUVEAU MANNER.
THOSE IN TOP ROW AND THE FIRST TWO IN THE SECOND ROW WERE
GOLD-LINED, THE OTHERS SILVER-LINED. THESE WERE PRODUCED IN THE
FIRST DECADE OF THIS CENTURY.

Most of the Unger ashtrays are prime examples of Art Nouveau of the early twentieth century. The author has seen very few examples of the style in ceramic or glass ashtrays.

Perhaps the most fertile of all fields related to smoking in which to collect Art Nouveau is that of match containers, variously termed safes and boxes.

Unger made some of these in silver in designs that matched its ashtrays but also made numerous other Art Nouveau designs in match safes with hinged tops. Altogether, fifty-two different designs are illustrated in the catalogue in the author's possession, all except one or two being in the Art Nouveau tradition. In addition to the flat-hinged boxes, Unger also made a few match holders that were footed. Three of these had sliding compartments for matches, one in the shape of an owl's head.

A number of other manufacturers also fashioned match safes in Art Nouveau decor. A group of these in silver was offered in a 1902 catalogue of Oskamp, Nolting & Company of Cincinnati at wholesale prices of $1.34 to $3.25. Some safes were made of pearl with metal bands decorated in the new art style. These had sterling silver tops and bases and were somewhat higher in price than those made entirely of sterling.

Almost every illustrated offering of groups of match safes in merchandise catalogues of the period mentioned included at least one or two adorned with lithe female nudes. Although a large percentage of these match safes were rectangular, others boasted curvilinear cases and tops.

In a closely allied category are cigarette cases. Some manufacturers issued matching cigarette cases and match safes in Art Nouveau designs. A set of this type, offered in the 1912 catalogue of Albert Brothers, listed the wholesale price of the cigarette case at $18 and the match box at $6. Both were of silver.

In the years when rolling one's own was popular, cigarette paper cases to hold the tissues in which the tobacco was rolled were produced for the more affluent males. Both the cigarette

MOROCCO LEATHER CIGAR CASES SHOWING
THE NEW ART INFLUENCE, CA. 1905.

GROUP OF STERLING SILVER CIGARETTE
CASES OFFERED FOR SALE IN 1907.

paper cases and the cigarette cases were similar in shape and designs. So, too, were cigar cases, although the latter were deeper to allow for the greater thickness of cigars. In the designs of all these cases, too, the female nude was popular in those languid, reclining poses.

Even cigar cutters, utilized for cutting off the tip of cigars to obviate the somewhat less sanitary method of biting them off, were made in the Art Nouveau style. These were fashioned of various metals, frequently silver or silver plate, and many were given a gold finish. The costlier ones were hand engraved.

In 1910, Wallenstein, Mayer & Company, Cincinnati wholesale jewelers, were offering boxed sets consisting of a match box and a pocket knife or of those two items plus a cigar cutter. The pieces were of sterling silver, and the cases were of leatherette lined with silk or velvet. Wholesale prices started at $4.75 for the two-piece sets and at $7.50 for those with three pieces.

Pipes were apparently neglected by most designers under the sway of Art Nouveau. A few were turned out with floral decorations in that style around the outside tops of the bowls. Several also put in their appearance with similar decorations on a gold-filled band joining together the stem and bottom extrusion of the bowl. Among these were some meerschaum types and a few French briars.

A quadruple-plated, gold-lined smoking set appeared in 1905 with a large tray holding an open cigar jar, a match holder, and an ashtray, all adorned with Art Nouveau tulips with very long stems molded to their exteriors.

Occupational shaving mugs have been popular with collectors for years, but the shaving brush itself has been neglected. Yet, a host of brushes with decorations in the new style appeared in the early 1900's. So did some shaving cups and soap boxes. The brushes had silver or plated handles graced with most of the types of commercial Art Nouveau decoration popular in this country. Some brushes were de-

FOUR-PIECE SMOKING SET, GOLD-LINED, PRODUCED EARLY IN THIS CEN-
TURY.

EVEN MEN'S SUSPENDERS DID
NOT ESCAPE THE ART NOU-
VEAU INFLUENCE.

TYPICAL OF COMMERCIAL ART
NOUVEAU IN THE UNITED
STATES EARLY IN THIS CEN-
TURY IS THIS MILITARY BRUSH.

signed so that the brush itself folded into the handle when not in use.

Unger Brothers made them in its own patterns with several matching soap boxes—round, with caps that could be pulled off. Other manufacturers marketed sets that consisted of an Art Nouveau mug and a plain-handled brush, occasionally decorated with beading, in sateen-lined boxes of leatherette. Most of these were silver-plated with wholesale prices in 1910 ranging from about $5 to $7. Gold-lined soap cups experienced a heyday in that and the next few years. Some cups were lined with glass. The majority were handled and some had a bracket attachment for holding the brush. There were Art Nouveau cups and brushes made in a pattern trade-marked "Hygenic." You may also wish to watch out for the new art designs on self-coiling razor straps, which largely passed out of existence after the perfection of the safety razor with its throw-away blades.

Art Nouveau pocket flasks of silver or silver plate were toted about early in the century by young men (and older ones, too) of some affluence. Capacities were from one-fourth of a pint to a pint. No less than is the case today, they found their way, neatly snuggled in hip or overcoat pockets, to football games, where surreptitious—and often not so surreptitious—nips were taken from them to ward off the autumn chill or wintry blasts. Flasks undoubtedly have been carried to football games since the first intercollegiate game was played in America at New Brunswick, New Jersey, in 1823 between Rutgers and Princeton.

Canes in a wide variety of shapes with solid gold or gold-filled heads were the fashion for males early this century, and the Art Nouveau style was not overlooked in the decoration of many of their round, oval, or crook-shaped heads. Leaf and flower predominated. The more elegant canes boasted ebony sticks, and the heads contained a small plate on which the owner's name or initials could be engraved. Canes of this type were fairly expensive, better ones being offered in 1905

A VARIETY OF SILVER UM-
BRELLA HANDLES, SUCH AS
THIS ONE BY UNGER, AS
WELL AS CANE HEADS WERE
MADE IN ART NOUVEAU
STYLES.

ART NOUVEAU'S INFLUENCE EX-
TENDED EVEN TO SUCH LOWLY OB-
JECTS AS THE SHOEHORN EARLY IN
THIS CENTURY. THE HANDLE IS SIL-
VER. *Unger Brothers.*

SILVER FLASKS SUCH AS THIS
ONE PREDATED THE PRO-
HIBITION ERA "HIP FLASKS"
BY MORE THAN A DECADE.
Unger Brothers.

at retail prices of as much as $80 or $90 with heads of gold. Even those with gold-filled heads were retailing for as much as $50, although less elaborate ones were available at half that price and some were offered as "seconds" at around $10 to $20.

Quite similar heads could be found on men's tight-rolling umbrellas. These had handles of ivory with gold-filled caps and bands; horn, boxwood, crabwood, buckhorn, or other woods with sterling silver trimmings; or sterling silver or gold-filled metal. Heads alone, without sticks or umbrellas, were also sold by manufacturers and jobbers.

Female heads and flowers with writhing stems were utilized for the tops of men's (and women's) celluloid dresser combs. The tops were often of sterling silver, and small celluloid combs of this type were selling in 1905 for as high as $30 each. Plain celluloid combs with celluloid tops (or backs), on the other hand, were retailing for as little as $1.25 to $2.

The turn of the century also saw the manufacture of folding pocket combs for men. These were housed in Art Nouveau cases of sterling silver. The cases were of two types: oblong with open tops, or hinged to the celluloid comb itself at one end. Unger produced its share of handsome silver cases for eyeglasses. Some had their top halves covered with alligator hide.

Other collectible objects in Art Nouveau commercial styles that will appeal particularly to men include bottle openers (some of sterling), bottle corks with silver heads, and corkscrews; pocket knives with cases that frequently housed such additional articles as nail files, nail scissors, and corkscrews; suspenders with silver buckles in styles similar to those on women's garters of the same period; wallets of morocco, alligator hide, seal, and walrus leathers with silver mountings and shields; numerous key rings, key tags, and bag checks; and tie clasps.

IX

Writing Accessories

Lovely inkwell of white glass created by René Lalique about 1910. *Courtesy, Musée des Arts Décoratifs, Paris.*

ART NOUVEAU DESIGN snuggled its way thoroughly into the broad field of writing accessories from inkstands to blotters made primarily or partly of metal.

Especially appealing are the little silver pencils manufactured in some profusion in this century's earlier years and the small sterling silver pencil cases. The cases were oval and oblong so that pencils could be fitted tightly inside. Most were only 2½ to 3 inches long, but a few measured nearly 4 inches in length. Some were open at one end with a cap on the opposite end, but others were two-part affairs that fitted together and inside of which small pencils were housed. Some of the open cases had erasers instead of metal caps on one end.

Most of the tiny charm pencils had rings at one end by which they could be attached to chatelaine or the shirt waist. They were about 2¾ to 3 inches in length. Some two-part pencils were made with threaded barrels so that the little pencils could be screwed into the case point-first when not in use or taken out and reversed when needed for writing.

Numerous sterling pencils of this type appeared with neatly chased Art Nouveau designs on the cases and/or pencil barrels. One popular brand was the Magic pencil, some of which were gold-plated and were wholesaling for $15 to $36 a dozen in 1904 and 1905.

Inkstands have been made through the decades in almost every shape and size conceivable. Silver-plated ones in Art Nouveau designs were being offered by Simpson, Hall, Miller

STERLING SILVER ERASER
LETTER OPENER, AND SEAL,
1905.

STERLING SILVER STAMP BOXES
SUCH AS THESE WHOLESALED
AT $8 TO $12 IN 1907.

PENCIL CASE OF STERLING
SILVER, FIRST DECADE OF
TWENTIETH CENTURY.

CHARMING INK STAND BY HOMAN
SILVER PLATE COMPANY, CA.
1906.

SILVER LETTER SEAL WITH ITS
UNDULATING LINES WOULD MAKE
A CHOICE ADDITION TO A COL-
LECTION OF COMMERCIAL ART
NOUVEAU. *Unger Brothers.*

ART NOUVEAU PEN RACK OF
PLATED SILVER IN A FRENCH
GRAY FINISH WAS OFFERED IN
1905 AT $2 WHOLESALE.

& Company early in the century. They were made in various shapes, some holding a single tiny glass well, others holding two glass wells or bottles, and some accompanied by matching stamp boxes, blotters, and pen racks. The wells had hinged silver-plated tops, also decorated by embossing. The company's trade appellations for its Art Nouveau stands included Vitiate, Whirligig, Visor, Visitor, Vista, and Veracity.

Several double inkstands (that is, with two bottles) and one or two single ones in modified Art Nouveau designs were made prior to 1920 by Reed & Barton. One single stand contained a well upon whose silver-plated top stood a female figure in flowing garment. An attractive double stand in the form of a footed tray held two wells of overlay glass with thumbprint cutting.

A delightful inkstand, depicting Pierrot arising from the center of a cluster of flower petals, was crafted in the early 1900's by Homan Silver Plate Company. The clown's head actually formed the handle of the inkstand top. Homan made other stands in Art Nouveau styles, as did several other silver-plate manufacturers. The glass wells were usually purchased from glass houses and then fitted with metal tops.

Those who eye inkstands for a collection may well want to take a look at pens and penholders, a few of which, early in this century, were chased with patterns quite reminiscent of Art Nouveau. These, too, were primarily floral.

Penholders were universally used in those years preceding the advent of the fountain pen. Some manufacturers made them of 14-karat gold plate with 14-karat gold points to accompany them. Ten-karat barrels and points were also produced to sell at slightly lower prices. The gold-plated holders of the higher-priced lines were decorated by chasing.

Penholders with their slip-in nibs came into fairly widespread use in the late 1820's and the fountain pen was beginning to sell in the 1880's, but even at the outbreak of the First World War these had by no means entirely supplanted the slip-in nib holders. Nevertheless, during the first decade of this century, the A. A. Waterman Company was offering a diversified line of fountain pens of the self-filling type with its own patented feeds. One of these with a sterling silver mounting fashioned in a style imitative of Art Nouveau had appeared by 1907. Such pens with chased bands definitely in the Art Nouveau manner were being marketed in 1915. Several of "Moore's non-leakable" fountain pens were among these. They had hard rubber barrels, some with applied filigree work, others chased or engraved. Moore also made a line of "tourist" fountain pens, which measured only 4½ inches in length when closed and could be conveniently carried in a gentleman's lower vest pocket or a lady's chatelaine bag. A few of these with Art Nouveau sterling silver open work on the barrels were offered.

Among other brands of fountain pens in the Art Nouveau style of decoration were the John Holland pens, patented on July 1, 1902. A particularly attractive one with sterling leaf filigree wholesaled for $8.75 or could be had with gold-filled leaf filigree for $10.

The slide holders for penholders were also made of pearl and ebony wood.

Trade names of Art Nouveau style fountain pens in addition to those named above included Autofiller, Gem, Faultless, Economy, and Crown.

The collector of writing accessories should not neglect the pen rack. Several versions of these decorated in the new art manner by embossing appeared in plated silver around 1905. Available, too, were writing sets consisting of an inkwell, blotter, eraser, seal, letter opener and penholder—or sometimes only three or four of these articles—in silk-lined cases covered with fancy paper. The better sets were made of sterling silver.

Rocker blotters with sterling or silver-plated tops and handles in the Art Nouveau manner were made by Simpson, Hall, Miller & Company, and others. Some of these had knobs and others open-work handles by which they were rocked across the wet ink. Also made in abundance were rolling blot-

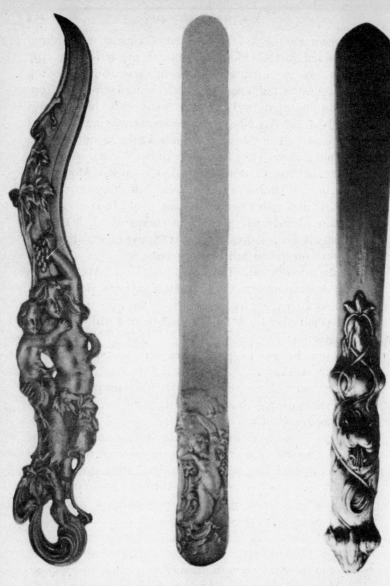

Three writing implements characteristic of flamboyant Art Nouveau design are an Unger Brothers paper cutter in sterling (left) with two figures whose legs terminate in cloven hooves, an Unger Brothers paper creaser in sterling (center) adorned with a voluptuous mermaid, and a letter opener (right) in Martelé by the Gorham Company.

ters with sterling or plated handles, and a few were produced with silver-trimmed pearl handles. The blotting paper was wrapped around a core held by brackets to the handle.

Letter openers, also called paper cutters, constitute a fertile field for the Art Nouveau collector. Some of the most delightful were crafted by Unger Brothers. These had steel shafts and silver handles or pearl shafts with silver handles. A collector's dream in this commercial field would be the Unger all-silver cutter with curved blade and handle decorated with a child clasping his mother, the latter bare from the waist up, her left hand clutching a bunch of grapes at the top of the blade. Unger also produced miniature-sized paper cutters that measured only 2¾ inches in length, and a line of flat-bladed paper creasers.

In some early twentieth-century merchandise catalogues the phrase "letter opener" was applied to an instrument with a semi-round blade and "paper cutter" to one with a much broader flat blade. Numerous letter openers and paper cutters were produced as pieces in a desk set that might consist of matching ink eraser, envelope moistener, and wax seal.

Bookmarks are among the most charming of small collectible objects, although they appear to be fairly scarce. Obviously, however, judging by advertisements of them in earlier years, they were once plentiful, and a large number of combination bookmarks paper cutters were made. The choicest, perhaps, are in sterling silver (if one excludes the Stevensgraphs, those woven marks that are not within the scope of this book) with Art Nouveau-type handles. Some bookmarks and some of the combinations appeared with cords and tassels. A bookmark with a handle in the shape of petals was available in 1907 as was another whose handle consisted of a cluster of lily-like flowers. One combination was produced with a handle in the form of leaves and berries.

In this field, Unger again was a leader in the Art Nouveau styles. This firm made small bookmarks of silver in at least a score of different designs. Handles of the smallest of these were in the form of flowers. Slightly larger ones had handles shaped as female heads. A few of the smaller ones were also made with animal heads forming the handles or tops.

A number of bookmarks were made of silk ribbons to the ends of which silver ornaments were attached, but the author has not located any of this type with Art Nouveau designs, although it is possible some were manufactured.

In 1915, Otto Young & Company offered a boxed assortment of half a dozen bookmarks with sterling silver tops, all of them in the commercial Art Nouveau fashion, at $4 an assortment. The same company had some in solid gold in 1907, the tip of one of which formed a lily with two leaves and stems.

Wax seals, once used for sealing letters, with the seal set in the lower end of a silver or silver-plated handle, were made in some fascinating shapes. An exceptionally fine one put out by Unger had a handle in the shape of a Madonna-like figure holding a bouquet of lilies and with additional lilies and undulating stems forming the lower part. The use of these seals is no longer in fashion, and more's the pity, because they were attractive. They once graced the writing tables of our ancestors, and many were carried about by travelers who wrote letters while away from home.

Very fine early seals were in the category of jewelry; some were set into rings. Their use extends back generations. Many of these signet rings were made of gemstones, carved with either crests or various other devices. Josiah Wedgwood once provided for desk use seals with his famous jasperware handles. The majority produced in this country late last century and early in the present one, however, were equipped with the metal handles. To use these seals, one gently heated the wax over a flame, then rubbed it on the envelope, and finally impressed the seal atop the wax. This could actually constitute something of a ceremony, but we live so breathlessly today that we rarely have time for ceremony.

WAVECREST LETTER HOLDER WITH METAL
MOUNTS PRODUCED EAR['] Y IN THIS CEN-
TURY BY THE C. F. MONROE COMPANY.
Author's collection.

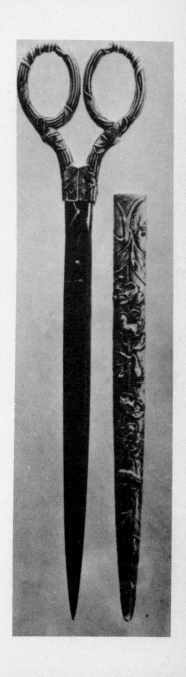

BANKER'S SHEARS AND SHEATH IN MAR-
TELÉ. *Courtesy, The Gorham Company.*

Finally, one may wish to look about for Art Nouveau paper and envelope racks and postcard holders. These appeared in silver, silver-plate, bronze, and other metals, frequently with cutout or open-work designs in the fronts and backs, fastened to bases that were sometimes footed. The postcard holders resembled, in miniature, the tin mail boxes once utilized on porches and had a compartment at the front for holding stamps.

X

Miscellaneous Table Accessories

Pewter goblets and tankard by Walter Scherj & Company, Nuremburg, Germany, ca. 1898. *Courtesy, Victoria and Albert Museum, London.*

OUR DINING TABLES TODAY, laden though they may be with food, are rarely as laden as were those of our ancestors with decorative accessories that somehow lent added zest to dining. Two or three generations ago, our grandparents and great-grandparents took special pains to grace their tables on Sundays, at parties, and at every large family gathering with center-pieces, including epergnes and beautiful fruit bowls. For such occasions they also broke out their treasured serving pieces ranging from decorated bread trays to handsome tureens.

Among the vessels and containers they often used and which are seldom seen today except in the antiques shops were handsome cruet sets, bonbon dishes, enameled and otherwise decorated water sets, nut bowls, and handpainted porcelain.

These did not entirely escape the short but potent influence of Art Nouveau. There were even baking dishes of plated silver with the familiar molded decorations of delicate flowers and stems around their base and tops. Wm. A. Rogers issued a plated bake dish whose top was adorned with molded vegetables. Another quadruple-plated dish had a top deco-rated with stylized petaled flowers and leaves. Simpson, Hall, Miller featured several elaborately decorated baking dishes with both tops and bases covered with floral motifs, some with asymmetrical handles.

An enormous variety of fruit bowls made of colored and decorated glasses in silver and silver-plated holders was put out over a period of years. These are extremely popular today,

SILVER-PLATED NAPKIN RING OFFERED IN 1905.

MUSTARD POT IN UNGER BROTHERS SILVER, 1906.

BERRY OR FRUIT BOWL OF ROSE GLASS ON PLATED STAND; MADE AROUND 1906 BY HOMAN SILVER PLATE COMPANY.

the smaller ones often being referred to as "brides' baskets." They made handsome gifts and were extremely attractive for use on the table. Many of the bases were quite ornate; some featured figures of cupids holding the bowl aloft; others had this chore performed by a lissome maiden. The glass bowls usually, but not always, had crimped edges. Some of the stands were handled; others were not.

The heyday of these delightful bowls was the first two decades of this century, although they were made both earlier and later, and they largely replaced the more cumbersome epergne as a table centerpiece.

Scores of berry dishes were turned out by such firms as Homan Manufacturing Company, Wm. A. Rogers, and E. G. Webster & Sons, most of whom manufactured the bases themselves but purchased the glass bowls from glass producers. The bowls appeared in a wide diversity of colors, in overlay, with enameling, and with gilding. Many were Bohemian and were imported into the United States in large quantities.

Berry bowls also were made entirely of metal, usually silver-plated. Homan Manufacturing Company produced one in the shape of a large leaf with a curved handle at one end and small feet. These were sometimes originally designated as "fruit or nut bowls," although other bowls, usually in plated silver, were designed specifically for nuts. The fruit bowls, incidentally, were used interchangeably for berries and sometimes were advertised as "fruit or berry bowls." Dual-use bowls, in fact, were abundant. One type was called a "nut or biscuit bowl." Simpson, Hall, Miller turned out plated nut bowls equally as lavish as its berry bowls.

Cruet sets and a variety of caster sets— some consisting only of salt and pepper shakers and others of additional bottles for oils and condiments of diverse kinds—bore Art Nouveau decor either on the containers or the plated stands, or both. Caster sets with cut bottles and plated stands with floral decorations embossed are desirable collectors' items. Many had

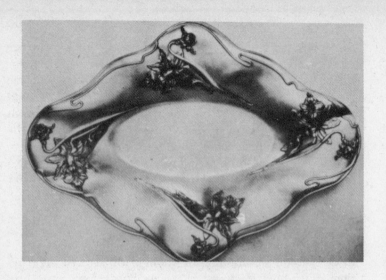

SILVER-PLATED BREAD TRAY, 14 INCHES LONG, WAS MADE BY
WILCOX SILVER PLATE COMPANY, MERIDEN, CONNECTICUT. *The
International Silver Company Historical Library.*

WILCOX SILVER PLATE COMPANY MADE THESE CAKE TRAYS IN
THE ART NOUVEAU STYLE. ONE ON LEFT IS 10 INCHES LONG. *The
International Silver Company Historical Library.*

elaborately fashioned handles by which they could be lifted. In view of current prices commanded by such sets, it is surprising to learn they wholesaled for as little as $3.50 with five bottles early in the century. Simpson, Hall, Miller offered a number of them in an early twentieth-century catalogue, along with one not of its own manufacture, commenting, "This caster [the word is spelled with either an *o* or an *e*] is single plate and does not bear our Trade Mark."

Individual salt and pepper shakers also appeared in both metal and glass (with metal tops), embellished with daisies and stylized flowers and other embossed or enamelled adornments beloved of the commercial Art Nouveau designer. A salt and pepper caster with a small footed holder in the Art Nouveau manner was made by Barbour Silver Plate Company. The containers were of decorated glass, featuring flowers and green leaves. Silver-plated pepper boxes with matching salts with exteriors covered with a profusion of flowers, vines, and leaves were produced by Simpson, Hall, Miller. Similar plated ones, though not so ornate, were offered in Wallenstein, Mayer & Company's 1910 catalogue.

Both silver and plated bread trays designed in numerous shapes have been manufactured for many years, as have those of glass. While there are numerous historical bread trays of glass still awaiting collectors and many others already in collections, glasshouses seem to have avoided the Art Nouveau fashion. Silver and silver-plating companies, on the other hand, did not. Plated trays measuring 10 to about 14 inches in length appeared with floral decor embossed around the edges and sometimes extending into the body of the tray itself. A good many such trays were used interchangeably for bread or cake, but some were embossed or engraved with the word "bread."

Some trays appeared with flowers and leaves or vines interlocked around the entire border. E. G. Webster & Sons and Homan Silver Plate Company were among the producers of these in the Art Nouveau style. They also turned out handled

THIS CONFECTION EPERGNE IN HIGH ART NOUVEAU DESIGN
WAS MANUFACTURED IN PLATED SILVER BY THE VICTOR
SILVER COMPANY, SHELTON, CONNECTICUT. IT IS 11 INCHES
TALL. *The International Silver Company Historical Library.*

THE DERBY SILVER COMPANY PRODUCED THIS WATER SET
IN ITS MARGUERITE PATTERN IN PLATED SILVER. THE GOB-
LET WAS GOLD-LINED. *The International Silver Company
Historical Library.*

cake baskets with quite similar embossing. The most fascinating of the cake baskets have handles also with Art Nouveau decorations. Some handles were pierced, others twisted into variations of the whiplash line. Some cake plates stood on solid bases and others had four small feet, the latter usually embossed.

In an allied category were the bonbon dishes mentioned earlier. Some really choice ones were fashioned in sterling silver with pierced work designs and in the form of miniature baskets with handles. The majority, however, were handleless. Most bonbon dishes were small, measuring just a few inches in length or diameter, and were crafted in both oval and oblong shapes. Should you mistake a bonbon dish for an almond dish, don't let it worry you. Although manufacturers labeled some of their small containers almond dishes, they were almost identical in appearance to the bonbon. Homan Silver Plate Company made a bonbon dish with raised flowers around the rim and two whiplash lines across the center of the bowl. Two sizes were available—$3\frac{1}{2}$ inches and $7\frac{1}{2}$ inches, and the former wholesaled at only 69 cents in 1907.

A fairly wide variety of water sets was on the market during the first decade of this century with decorations in the new art styles. Of these the most fascinating were the tilting sets, consisting of a silver or plated pitcher on a stand with accompanying stemmed and footed goblets. These pitchers, nearly all of them elaborately embossed or engraved, tilted forward on their stands for pouring. The large tilting sets were relatively expensive 65 or 70 years ago and were apparently treasured not only by their original purchasers but also by their descendants, so that not too many of them are around today in antiques shops. Those whose plate has badly worn are usually worth replating.

Less affluent families usually managed with plated water sets consisting of an individual pitcher and matching footed goblets, plus a "waiter" tray in oval and oblong shapes. Interestingly, the majority of these sets contained only a single goblet; some were available with what was referred to in earlier days as a slop, or slop bowl. Because the gold color appealed to our ancestors, many such sets were gold-lined.

Simpson, Hall, Miller identified the offerings in its catalogues with code names, some of which seem indeed incongruous. For example, various items of its water sets were identified by such key names as Unmanly, Unready, Unpleasant, Unruly, Unwilling, Unlawful, and Unsafe!

Pitchers for the water sets were fashioned in a wide variety of shapes, as were their handles. Occasionally, instead of a goblet, the water set came with a tumbler. These were much cheaper than the footed goblets, some wholesaling in silverplate for as little as 50 cents. Many water pitchers, of course, were offered as individual items and matching tumblers and waiter trays could be purchased separately.

In an allied category are wine coolers and ice pails, the bulk of which were silver-plated. Wine coolers were made with either ring handles or a bail handle. Most stood on a flat base, but the collector will occasionally encounter one on small feet.

Art Nouveau had its effect on certain decorators of white porcelain. Its impact, however, seems to have been greater on amateurs who bought porcelain white blanks to decorate as a leisure-time occupation in their homes than upon professional china painters. From time to time, one is likely to find in the shops plates, bowls, and other articles of good-quality porcelain with Art Nouveau decoration obviously done by gifted amateurs and with the painting not infrequently over the glaze.

Nevertheless, during the first decade of the century some potteries did produce handpainted porcelain in the Art Nouveau manner with emphasis on flowers and/or foliage done in soft colors but almost invariably with gold trimmings. Most abundantly in evidence were plates, berry and other bowls, olive dishes, and vases. Prices of these varied according to the quality of the porcelain and of the decoration, as they should today. Some of the high-quality blanks for home decoration came from the Haviland factories in Limoges, France, others from various potteries around the United States. Thayer & Chandler of Chicago was a major purveyor of white porcelain for decorating 60 or 70 years ago. The company continues in business today.

Some of these handpainted pieces were quite attractive and were hung on walls for decorative purposes. In fact, a good many plaques were made especially for this purpose. Such pieces whose decoration still remains good can add charm to almost any room in the present-day home.

Many silver-plated and silver cups and mugs with Art Nouveau decor were made between 1905 and 1915. The 1910 catalogue of A. Hirsch & Company illustrates several children's heavily silver-plated cups with engraved and chased decorations of rather broad whiplash lines. These had French gray exteriors and were gold-lined inside.

Other cups and mugs bore satin engraved stylized flowers, leaves, and tendrils. Some handles were also embossed with flowers.

Fern dishes filled with cool, green fronds not only stood atop the once-popular fern stands in the homes of our grandparents but often graced the dining table as well after the dishes had been cleared. Made of both metals and porcelain or glazed earthenware, these containers were usually oval-shaped and many were footed. Silver-plated fern dishes (sometimes referred to as ferners) with Art Nouveau embossed designs were made by Homan Silver Plate Company early in the century. Although customarily the decoration was around the side of the dishes, Homan produced one with what it termed "raised fancy flowers" that extended beyond the top of the bowl. Metal fern dishes usually had porcelain liners, although occasionally glass was used, and handles were attached to the liners so they could be easily lifted out. Simpson, Hall, Miller made one Art Nouveau fern dish (which it called a fern coaster) code-named Verger and another called Wept.

The Forbes Silver Company numbered among its new art productions a handsome chased fern dish whose flowers had long, waving stems and whose lining could be either white or green crockery.

Some fern dishes measured only 4½ inches in diameter but others ranged up to diameters of 10 or 11 inches. Reed & Barton manufactured one elaborate fern dish with plated lining in high Art Nouveau style, complete with female head but with paw feet.

Collectors should bear in mind that whereas the pioneers of Art Nouveau strove most earnestly for a full break with tradition and the styles of the past, the break was rarely complete, and in commercial Art Nouveau designers often deliberately incorporated a traditional stylistic feature, such as the paw foot just mentioned, within the framework of the new style. Incongruity, therefore, is often a hallmark of commercial Art Nouveau.

XI

Candlesticks and Candelabra

STRICTLY ART NOUVEAU IS THIS CANDELABRUM PRODUCED BY MERIDEN BRITANNIA COMPANY, ONE OF THE COMPANIES FORMING THE INTERNATIONAL SILVER COMPANY. *The International Silver Company Historical Library.*

THE READER may wonder why an entire chapter should be devoted to Art Nouveau candlesticks and candelabra. The reason is simple: there is available today for the collector an almost fantastic array of these decorative utilitarian objects which were turned out in prodigious quantities during the first two decades of this century. Moreover, they lent themselves admirably to Art Nouveau treatment, not only through the application of decoration but also through the manipulation of the form itself.

Chances are that virtually all the silver makers and the manufacturers of silver-plate produced some candlesticks and candelabra, and some of them certainly issued tremendous quantities. They are therefore not scarce, but, because they can be utilized in so many areas of decor in today's homes and because there is a continuing demand for them, the more desirable ones are far from inexpensive.

Gorham made them in its Martelé line in numerous sizes and forms. They were squat and tall, dumpy and lean. There were Martelé candlesticks with saucers in the shapes of leaves, the base of the receptacle ending as a coiled snake, and the candle receptacle itself in lily form. These were accompanied by silver snuffers in bell shapes. Stick vase shapes were popular in this line. One handled candlestick was made with a very wide mouth surrounding the candle receptacle and an unusually broad and flaring base.

Another Martelé candlestick of the chamber type boasted silver leaves around the top of the receptacle and a saucer with scalloped partitions reminiscent of oyster plates. The

CANDLESTICK LABELED
"ART NOUVEAU" AND OF-
FERED IN PLATED SILVER
IN 1918; HEIGHT 8 INCHES.

SILVER-PLATED CANDELA-
BRUM OF 1905 FEATURED
FIVE LIGHTS ON RATHER
TORTURED STEMLIKE SUP-
PORTS.

ART NOUVEAU CANDLESTICKS IN MARTELÉ. *The Gorham Company.*

snuffer sat atop a snakelike handle. Flower forms provided the receptacle for others. These were marked with the Gorham fleur-de-lis.

Unger Brothers also produced some highly intriguing candlesticks graced with sterling flowers whose tendrils encircled the outside of the sticks. Some had flower form receptacles for the candles. In addition, Unger manufactured small oval candleholders of the chamber stick type with the receptacle on the rim.

Multi armed candelabra were turned out in a great diversity of designs, the arms lending themselves admirably to Art Nouveau interpretations. Often, their receptacles were in the shape of full-blown flowers. Homan Silver Plate Company manufactured several of this type. Barbour Silver Plate Company made a tall five-light candelabrum, whose receptacles were covered with flowers and sinuous leaves and vines. It stood on a base that rolled upward at four corners. The piece was topped in the center with a flame of plated silver that stood 17 inches above the base. Barbour also made one in the same design with three lights that measured 14 inches in height. This design was obviously a popular one, for it was made over a period of years.

Reed & Barton designed a two-arm electric candelabrum 16½ inches tall in the Art Nouveau style. The device, its bulb shafts capped with shades in the form of leaves, was actually a three-light candelabrum, since, in addition to the receptacles on the arms, there was one mounted on the much higher center shaft. A similar design for electric bulb use was made with five lights and was also utilized for single candlesticks. Reed & Barton produced several other candelabra with decoration in the Art Nouveau manner, including undulating arms.

Another manufacturer was Simpson, Hall, Miller & Company, among whose productions was a squat candelabrum that measured only 7½ inches tall and had four intertwined arms. As was the case with this company's other silver-plated wares, its candelabra, for the most part, abounded in embossed decorations, chiefly flowing lines, flowers, and leaves. The company put out an interesting line of candlesticks, too, including chamber candlesticks with snuffers of the conical type. One of the latter was coded Whynot.

A flame made of plated silver serving as the receptacle for the center shaft of early twentieth-century candelabra was obviously popular with the public for it is encountered time and again in trade catalogues.

A five-light candelabrum with a typical Art Nouveau shaft of quadruple silver-plate was offered for sale in 1907 and may have been made earlier. The shaft, though molded of a single piece of metal, gave the appearance of having been made of three pieces, two of them separated at the top from the center post so that they gave the impression of arms akimbo on a gaunt, headless figure.

As mentioned earlier, Art Nouveau mantel clocks were sometimes designed with an accompanying pair of either candelabra or candlesticks, and a large percentage of these were gold-plated.

Commercial candlesticks in the new art styles often featured shafts in designs that were part open work and that stood upon a base supported by sinuously curving legs decorated with additional curves of plated silver. Some legs were folded upward from the base to join the body of the shaft about one-third of the way up.

One plated candlestick, 9 inches tall, was made in the shape of a woman, supporting the receptacle with her upraised arms, whose lower garment showed folds that were whiplash variations. Another, gold-plated, had sturdy flower stalks entwined around the central shaft but separated from it at several points.

One called "Art Nouveau" and offered in 1918 had a receptacle in the shape of an opened lily, a shaft in the form of a broad, undulating lily stalk, and a base made of four leaves.

It was available in either a blue or bronze finish, stood 8 inches tall, and wholesaled for only $2. Still another candlestick of 1918 vintage and also heralded as "Art Nouveau" combined floral decor with draped bands that are reminiscent of the Adam style. It, too, was available in a blue or a bronze finish.

Shafts and bases of many candlesticks of the 1905–1920 period were embossed with lines that played variations on the whiplash.

In 1902, there were gold-plated candlesticks whose shafts were formed as an undulating curve of stalk with leaves, with downturned leaves around the base of the candle receptacle. Standing on one side of the base and clutching the center of the stalk-shaft was a winged cupid. The receptacle itself was in the form of an opened flower.

Although many objects were fashioned in the commercial Art Nouveau manner through the first three decades or so of this century, not many are in greater supply today than candlesticks and candelabra. But scarce, indeed, are the individually crafted sticks and candelabra created by noted Art Nouveau craftsmen and artists, often for the interior decoration of houses they themselves designed. Most of these have already found their way into museums or private collections or are preserved in homes of the period.

The choicer silver pieces certainly include those in Gorham's Martelé and those made by Unger Brothers. The available silver-plated items are much less expensive and, if their silver coat is in good condition, they can be most interesting acquisitions. Despite the demurrer of certain purists, sticks and candelabra whose silver is badly worn are much more attractive when replated. That way, too, they can serve a useful purpose in today's homes. It is better, however, to pass by those that have been badly damaged through the years. Proper restoration may cost more than it is worth.

XII

Art Nouveau Furniture

INLAID WORK TABLE, 1900, BY EMILE GALLÉ. *Photograph by courtesy of the Victoria and Albert Museum, London.*

THE INROADS of Art Nouveau into the realms of furniture and interior decoration culminated in some creations that bordered on the exotic and evidenced the strong influence of Japanese design on the new art.

Furniture, in particular, reflects the positive reaction of new style designers against the dominance and restraint of tradition. Some pieces give the impression that their Art Nouveau conceivers and craftsmen sought not so much to create something new, as to avoid creating *anything* that obtained authority from the past.

Connoisseurs have said that the emphasis in Art Nouveau furniture was upon functionalism, and to an extent this appears true. Yet, if functionalism and comfort are allied, then certainly numerous pieces of furniture—particularly chairs and settees—in the new style left something to be desired. Vigor keynotes some pieces, but it is a stark vigor and in contrast to the delicacy of Art Nouveau design in other fields.

On the other hand, a variety of pieces exist that are graceful, charming, and, in their own way, even demure. These include small writing desks, screens, and vitrines. There are definite distinctions between furniture created in what is known as the High Art Nouveau style and that crafted in the later geometrical or cubic versions and based upon straight lines and right angles whose rigidity is tempered by contours in the surface decoration.

It must be recognized that not all Art Nouveau craftsmen

FIRE SCREEN BY EMILE GALLÉ, 1900. *Courtesy of the Victoria and Albert Museum, London.*

VITRINE IN THE ART NOUVEAU MANNER DESIGNED BY GEORGES DE FEURE, PARIS (1899–1900), AND FASHIONED OF WALNUT. *The Metropolitan Museum of Art, Edward C. Moore, Jr., Gift Fund, 1926.*

COLUMBIA GRAND GRAFANOLA PHONOGRAPH, ELECTRIC MODEL, DATED AROUND 1912 IN SHAPE OF A MINIATURE GRAND PIANO AND WITH QUEEN ANNE-TYPE LEGS, MADE BY AMERICAN GRAPHO-PHONE COMPANY TO RETAIL AT $500. *Lightner Museum, St. Augustine, Florida.*

were dilettantes or recluses recoiling from an increasingly industrialized world in which the machine largely dictated to the man. Many were practical artisans, who, while striving for a new style, were also fully aware that they had clients as well as themselves to please.

In the furniture created in the High Art Nouveau style, asymmetry is frequently achieved in both contour and decor; and even in much of the furniture characterized by squarish or rectilinear lines, the exterior surfaces suggest motion or suppleness, and the winding line or the convolution is encountered in carving or applied ornamentation, particularly on such objects as tables, fire screens, cabinets, and clock cases. The majority of furniture in the new style might be characterized as definitely feminine in aspect, as were the majority of accessories utilized in interior decoration in general, from lamps to wall panels. Exceptions include the harsher—but never severely harsh—outlines of cubic Art Nouveau.

Some extraordinary furniture in the new style was created by that Frenchman of so many talents, Émile Gallé. Many of his pieces were decorated with flowers of inlaid veneers, and some bore quotations from writers—poets in particular— whom he admired. This was the same device he had employed on numerous pieces of his glass and pottery.

Among his furniture productions were fire screens with graceful contours. One in the Bethnal Green Museum in London is made of ash, its surface decoration featuring carved clusters of leaves with long, winding stems and tendrils extending upward to join additional carved leaves in the center of the top and one tendril extending downward to join a carving at one side of a curved base. The legs, which are an extension of the screen's borders, almost appear to sprawl.

A Gallé worktable of ash, in the same museum, made in 1900—four years before his death—has elaborately carved flower whorls, whose stems, gracefully intertwined, extend the table's length and become a part of the end supports. A workbox beneath a rectangular top is inlaid and is partly supported by asymmetrical carvings.

ART NOUVEAU CABINET BY LOUIS MAJO-
RELLE OF FRANCE, 1897–1900. *Courtesy,
Victoria and Albert Museum, London.*

DESK OF AFRICAN AND OLIVE ASH BY HECTOR GUIMARD DATES ABOUT 1903. IT IS 28¾ INCHES HIGH AND 101 INCHES WIDE. *Collection, The Museum of Modern Art, New York City, gift of Mme. Hector Guimard.*

ART NOUVEAU TABLE DESIGNED BY EDWARD COLONNA, OF FRANCE, IS MADE OF PALISANDER WOOD. *The Metropolitan Museum of Art, Edward C. Moore, Jr., Gift Fund, 1926.*

Furniture of remarkable grace was also produced by Louis Majorelle and Alexandre Charpentier. Some of the designs for marquetry on furniture by Majorelle, a co-founder with Gallé of the École de Nancy, were done by Victor Prouvé.

A six-foot-tall cabinet by Majorelle in which veneer patterns are combined with metal decorations is also in the Bethnal Green Museum. Examples of Charpentier's work can be seen in Museé des Arts Décoratifs in Paris.

Hector Guimard, remembered particularly for his entrances to the Paris metro stations, also turned to furniture and interior decoration. A striking case for a tall clock which he made is now preserved in Musée des Arts Décoratifs, and a desk of ash marked by flowing lines that once graced his own home was presented by his wife to the Museum of Modern Art in New York City. Guimard also made upholstered chairs with the tall, supple backs characteristic of much of this period and with lines from which movement seems to flow. An exaggeration of proportion is a feature that typifies numerous pieces of Art Nouveau furniture, especially chairs and tables. Wood does not afford the same fluidity of handling as molten glass and pottery pastes, and its relative intractability must have been something of a harassment to designers who wanted to express liquidity of form in its framework. The compromise was to incorporate the curvilinear design elements on its flat surfaces. Perhaps a part of the reason for Louis Majorelle's success with Art Nouveau furniture was his method of procedure: he first modeled his pieces in clay.[1]

Among the names most prominently associated with furniture in the Art Nouveau manner is that of Charles Rennie Mackintosh. Like so many of the artists working in the new style, he, too, was a man of many talents—artist, architect, designer of furniture and furnishings. Born in Dennistoun, Glasgow, in 1868, he studied at the Glasgow School of Art and subsequently became associated with the architectural firm of Honeyman and Keppie. In the 1890's Mackintosh's design for the Glasgow School of Art was accepted—a major triumph for him. The primary part of this striking structure represents an outstanding example of the geometric Art Nouveau architectural style.

In 1897, Mackintosh collaborated with George Walton in furnishing and decorating one of Miss Cranston's Tea Rooms in Glasgow—a project that focused considerable attention on his talents. The manner in which the tea room was decorated represented what was to become known as the "Glasgow School style." This was entirely apart from the style of the École de Nancy. Recognition of his version of the new style that broke so sharply with tradition was more widespread on the European continent than in his own country.

Several Scottish artists in addition to Walton became associated with Mackintosh in the development of one phase of the late Art Nouveau style. Ornamentation of the surfaces was of prime importance to this group. Mackintosh created furniture ranging from chairs to highboys and also designed such furnishings and accessories as candelabra, lamps, fireplaces, and wall hangings. One of his contributions to the new style was the marriage of symmetry and asymmetry—a feature found not only in his furniture, but in his architectural designs as well.

In much of his furniture and accessories a sort of vertical angularity mingles with contours that mellow the starkness of sheer angularity. A chair he created at the turn of the century has an excessively tall and angular back frame, within which he set a solid back that tapered from the seat frame to the top rail, but ever so lightly, and with curvilinear ornamentation at the top. The seat itself is angular with straight front rails and straight round front legs, but the back legs consist of almost triangular-shaped yet slightly curved boards, joined by straight rails.

Other Mackintosh chairs also focus upon angularity, broken only by such features as a curved cutout in the top back rail or a flat splat curved on one end to join the back rails below the seat. He made tables with wide legs that tapered slightly from top to bottom and were decorated only with square cutouts. These same cutouts appeared on rails and backs of chairs and settees.

This, then, was the geometric or the cubic type of Art Nouveau furniture that was most characteristic of the Glasgow school, and it was also typical of the Vienna school just before the turn of this century. It was a distinct departure from the earlier curvilinear style.

Although most of Mackintosh's furniture was rectilinear and relatively simple in construction as well as in form, it fitted admirably into his overall room designs. Probably most of the decorative elements in the Mackintosh interiors were contributed by his wife, Margaret Macdonald Mackintosh, and her sister, Frances Macdonald. This at least is the view of Greta Daniel, an authority on his work.[2] The Macdonald sisters were leading figures in the Glasgow School of Art Nouveau.

Englishmen in addition to those already mentioned who produced or designed furniture and/or furnishings in the new style included the architect Charles Annesley Voysey and Arthur Heygate Mackmurdo, who influenced Voysey's style. And in the United States there was, of course, the indefatigable Louis Comfort Tiffany and his associates in Associated Artists, who decorated numerous homes of distinction.

On the European continent, other prominent figures in the Art Nouveau movement who created furniture and/or furnishings, in addition to their projects in other media, included the Belgians Victor Horta and Henri van de Velde; the Dutch architect Hendrik Petrus Berlage; the Frenchmen Eugène Colonna, Georges de Feure, and Claude Ferdinand Gaillard; the German exponents of *Jugendstil* August Endell, Bernard Pankok, and Richard Riemerschmid; and Antonio Gaudí y Cornet in Spain, who attained worldwide fame for his architectural achievements, particularly for his work with metal.

A chaise longue and chairs for an artist's loge by Louis Majorelle, of Nancy, France.

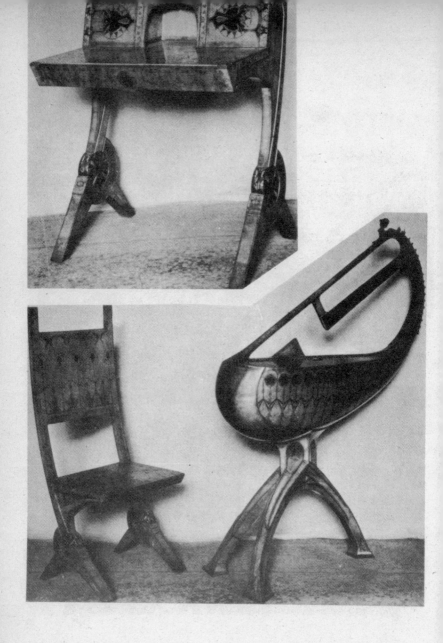

A desk, folding chair, and a fantastic tool kit by Charles Bugatti were shown at the Paris Beaux-Arts Exposition in 1904.

It should be borne in mind, as has been emphasized earlier, that many individuals who were architects by profession either designed furniture and furnishings themselves for the homes and emporia they built or had these designed under their supervision. Several of these are mentioned above.

A catalogue of decorative art displayed at the Beaux-Arts Exposition in Paris in 1904 is a treasure-house of illustrative information on Art Nouveau furniture of that period and its decorative adjuncts as well as its designers.

The catalogue, edited by Armand Guérinet, and published by the Librairie d'Art Décoratif, Paris, reveals that the work of Louis Majorelle was substantially represented, including such pieces as a work cabinet, bookcase, bureau, fauteuil and other chairs, chaise longues, canape, a piano with marquetry, tabouret and other types of tables, a large looking glass illuminated by lights at its base, and various storage and display cabinets.

The architectural firm of Sauvage and Sazarin displayed an arrangement of chairs, cabinets, a chaise longue, and other pieces plus wall decorations, all designed by Majorelle for an artist's loge. Ferdinand Bienvenu contributed a banquette (a long bench), whose seat could be lifted to disclose storage space and with an elaborately carved and curving top rail. A fascinating child's bed that resembled a cradle in construction except for rigid supports instead of rockers was exhibited by Auguste Raguel.

There were also intriguing secretaries by Albert Angst, beds by Maurice Dufréne and others, a fantastic armoire of ash and olive wood by Sauvage and Sazarin, chimney pieces by Eugene Bourdet and Alphonse Gentil, and others, an instrument box on legs with a handle in the shape of a saw by Charles Bugati, folding screens by Mme. d'Ernys, and other such accouterments of the home as music cabinets, dining tables, a combination divan-bookcase, vitrines, and decorative wall panels.

The outstanding American architect (and one of the relatively few) who worked in what was at least very close to the Art Nouveau style was Louis Sullivan, who had become exposed to the movement while studying and working in Paris prior to beginning his practice in Chicago.

Sullivan's predilection toward a new style appeared in some of his early work, including the Rothschild Department Store in Chicago which he designed as early as 1881, but his major work reflecting this influence flowered later with his plans and designs for structures such as the Guaranty Building in Buffalo, New York, and Carson Pirie Scott & Company's store in Chicago, in which a close affinity for certain Art Nouveau forms is clearly apparent.

Furniture manufacturers in the United States, except in a few rather isolated instances, found the new style of little interest in their commercial productions and chose instead to turn out reproductions and adaptations of eighteenth-century furniture, some monstrous versions of Empire pieces, heavy and square Mission furniture, and an assorted miscellany that included appalling concepts of the Edwardian, most of which tend today to make one's hair stand on end.

A few Art Nouveau concepts did creep into some of the designs of the Continental Manufacturing Co. of Chicago about the turn of this century, but they give the impression of designers casting about desperately for something just a little different from what their competitors had dreamed up. Continental turned out some walnut and oak lounges incorporating large shell forms in their backs or at the elevated end. A few also incorporated asymmetrical carved foliage in pierced backs. At least two of the company's bed-lounges featured a huge back cresting in the shape of a winged beetle. Art Nouveau naturalistic motifs also crept into some of the company's divan and chair backs, and in some backs of the latter the torturous Art Nouveau curve predominates.

Another Chicago manufacturer, J. S. Ford, Johnson & Co., flirted briefly and something less than tempestuously with Art Nouveau around 1901, turning out some chairs in oak,

MUSIC CABINET IN MAHAGONY BY
GEORGES TURCK, FRANCE.

ELECTRIC FIREPLACE FOR AN ART-
IST'S LOGE BY SCHEIDECKER AND
REGIUS OF FRANCE, 1904.

birch, and maple with tall, somewhat sinuously curved backs that were approximations of some of the European and British chairs. Their heavily stretchered legs, however, gave them an incongruous appearance.

A little rustic furniture in Art Nouveau styles appeared early this century, among its producers being the Old Hickory Chair Co. of Grand Rapids, Michigan—an area that was to reign for a good many years as the country's furniture capital. As the company's name indicates, its furniture was made entirely of hickory, and adaptations of Art Nouveau forms were found in a rather wide range of its productions, including chairs, settees, various tables, and bedroom furniture.

By and large, however, the masses of Americans early in this century had little or no interest in Art Nouveau furniture. As a result, American-made pieces are scarce. Occasionally, however, pieces from Great Britain and Europe wend their way to our larger auctions or become otherwise available from estates. Today these are being examined anew and with growing curiosity by the descendents of those who less than three-quarters of a century ago so largely ignored them. The result is that interesting pieces are likely to bring prices that will be increasing over the coming years.

Of the Art Nouveau furniture made in England, fairly sizable quantities were exported by furniture companies including J. S. Henry, William Birch, and Liberty's in the late nineteenth century, most of which is of a quality that will appeal to the discriminating collector. Other companies produced novelty pieces that depended for their Art Nouveau character chiefly on inlaid designs.

XIII

Graphic Arts and Sculpture

LITHOGRAPH, "MEDÉE THEATRE DE LA REN-
AISSANCE SARAH BERNHARDT," DONE BY AL-
PHONSE MUCHA IN 1898, MEASURES 81½ BY
30 INCHES. *The Collection, The Museum of
Modern Art, New York City, gift of Joseph H.
Heil.*

IN NO AREA is there more confusion about Art Nouveau than in that of the graphic arts, and the reason for it is that what is sometimes called the Aesthetic Movement and what is sometimes referred to as proto-Art Nouveau anticipated and led to Art Nouveau proper, so that lines of demarcation are blurred.

Numerous artists anticipated stylistic features of Art Nouveau, and, of course, even during the short years when the latter flourished, many artists worked in other styles; some worked in both Art Nouveau and their own individualistic modes. William Blake, that mystical engraver, painter, and poet, Dante Gabriel Rossetti, the individualistic poet and painter, and Walter Crane, that most prolific of Englishmen, were among those in whose work features of Art Nouveau are found—even though Crane was one of the new movement's most vocal critics. Japanese art had a profound influence upon both the Aesthetic Movement and Art Nouveau, and the former adopted the peacock, the lily, and the sunflower as its symbols; these were the elements that, in flowing line, became intimately associated with Art Nouveau.

Elements of Art Nouveau were also anticipated by or incorporated into work by such world-famous artists as Paul Gauguin, James McNeill Whistler, and Henri de Toulouse-Lautrec, though none was truly part and parcel of the Art Nouveau movement. And though William Morris and his associates inaugurated their own revolt in the world of practical and applied arts, rebelling against the vulgarity of mass

ATALANTA — A DESIGN
FOR A POSTER BY AUBREY
BEARDSLEY.

ILLUSTRATION BY WILL H. BRADLEY
FOR THE CHICAGO "SUNDAY TRIB-
UNE" AS PUBLISHED IN "THE STU-
DIO" FOR FEBRUARY, 1895.

BOOKPLATE DESIGN BY
HAROLD NELSON AS
PUBLISHED IN "THE STU-
DIO'S" SPECIAL WINTER
NUMBER, 1898–99.

production and the machine, some of their concepts were linked closely with and helped lead to many of the concepts of Art Nouveau.

Those interested in the roots of Art Nouveau and its precedents will find an excellent exposition of them in Robert Schmutzler's *Art Nouveau* and in Elizabeth Aslin's more recently published *The Aesthetic Movement: Prelude to Art Nouveau.*

The "high priest" of pictorial Art Nouveau was Aubrey Beardsley, who died at the age of 26 of tuberculosis in 1898, but who, during his prolific years, created work that shocked, outraged, and delighted the populace of his native England and all those abroad who encountered his drawings.

Like Oscar Wilde, whose books he illustrated, Beardsley was a fop and obviously an artist whose work frequently was designed to shock the observer. He was a friend of Sir Edward Burne-Jones, whose work influenced his own, and, if not a friend of, was at least influenced by Whistler as well as by the work of Japanese artists.

The great bulk of Beardsley's production consisted of black-and-white drawings featuring sinuous ornamentation and conveying marked sensuality and a sense of the bizarre, the exotic, and the fantastic. He made extraordinary use of the undulating curve and the juxtaposition of ornament and space.

Beardsley's early drawings published in *Studio* magazine and his illustrations for Thomas Malory's *Morte d'Arthur*, in an edition published by J. M. Dent about 1892, brought him almost instant recognition—and at the virtually precocious age of 20. Dent's chief executive, John Dent, had been seeking an illustrator to prepare striking line-block plates for the Malory classic, and of the line block Beardsley was truly master. The line block was a zinc etching produced by photo-mechanical means. No intermediate tones were possible in the line block, and to overcome or circumnavigate this limitation the artist utilized dark masses, outlines, and dots that helped create visual images of immense impact and excitement. Subsequently, Beardsley's work was published in *The Yellow Book,* of which he became art editor in early 1894; in *The Savoy,* for which he subsequently worked; in special editions of Oscar Wilde's *Salome* (1894), Alexander Pope's *The Rape of the Lock, Lysistrata,* and other books; as well as for other media, including posters.

Some of Beardsley's work has been compared to photographic negatives in which expanses of white space are found placed in relationship to dark or black areas so that this very relationship of white to black space takes on significance and, in fact, becomes vital to the total effect. Through the years a good many critics have characterized Beardsley's work as wicked, erotic, lustful, degenerate, eccentric—and much of it was: yet it also was beautiful in the sense of intellectual beauty, and though it almost never imparted warmth, its appeal was akin to that of chiseled marble.

Beardsley became the master of the sensuous and sensitive line that strayed lustfully into decorative ornamentation, like that encountered in his frontispiece for *Venus and Tannhauser* and his illustrations for *The Rape of the Lock,* but he also produced remarkable effects with a minimum of lines as some of his posters and book covers reveal.

It is little wonder that Beardsley's work shocked Victorian morality, and after his own conversion to Catholicism, the artist himself had deep doubts about what he had achieved, requesting before his death in 1898 that his pornographic work be destroyed. His wish was not fulfilled, and some of these drawings have recently been reissued.

The revival of popularity of Beardsley's work was reflected in a showing in 1966 at the Victoria and Albert Museum in London, which drew an attendance of more than 150,000 persons, and in another exhibition in 1967 at the Gallery of Modern Art in New York City.

Beardsley's work is identified by the initials "A.V.B." or the use of the name "Aubrey V. Beardsley" on the earlier drawings, and his later work was signed either "A.B." or simply "Aubrey Beardsley."

Beardsley's art was widely imitated, but most of the imitations pale by comparison with the original. Among the leading disciples of his style in this country were William H. Bradley, Ethel Reed, and Frank Hazenflug.

Art Nouveau represented a rebellion not only against historicism but against the academic style of working, which included painting on easels. The majority of artists who adopted the new style preferred instead to confine their painting to large panels that were predominantly decorative. Not only the easel but also the traditional picture frame was largely discarded.

The fluid forms that characterize so much Art Nouveau graphic work—the tendril, the stem, the bud—symbolize the artist's search for the roots of creation of life: the superficial depiction of life and of nature was considered contemptible. A painting was looked upon as something that should be useful, should make a contribution to whatever environment it became a part of, and, in brief, should be an integral part of the total decorative effect in its surroundings.

Surface decoration became predominant, and thin, pale colors became the choice. Space itself was utilized in a dramatic way. Greta Daniel puts it this way: "A curvilinear movement and . . . a combination of shadowless flat shapes. . . . These shapes given a highly evocative outline, cut into the surrounding space in such a way that the space too became a shape."

Frames gave way to panels, and these were occasionally further decorated to provide an embossed or relief effect by the addition of certain materials that extended above and beyond the flat surfaces.

A number of artists who began as painters switched, under the compelling influence of Art Nouveau, to allied creative fields, and Art Nouveau elements crept into the work of painters of other schools. Names to watch out for among the artists who worked in the new mode include Félix Vallotton.

ONE OF TOULOUSE-LAUTREC'S FA-
MOUS JANE AVRIL POSTERS. *The
Metropolitan Museum of Art, Harris
Brisbane Dick Fund, 1932.*

THE SMALL INITIALS "CR" AT THE
BOTTOM RIGHT-HAND CORNER OF
THIS DRAWING IDENTIFY IT AS THE
WORK OF CHARLES RICKETTS. THIS
WAS PUBLISHED IN "THE STUDIO"
IN OCTOBER, 1896.

actually a member of the Nabis school but who nevertheless often worked in both the mood and the mode of Art Nouveau, the Italian Giovanni Segantini, and others who have been mentioned earlier in this book as artists in more fields than one, among them Jan Toorop, Henri van de Velde, Edvard Munch, Max Klinger, Gustav Klimt, Charles Ricketts, Otto Eckmann, Peter Behrens, Ludwig von Hofmann, and Frances and Margaret Macdonald.

The use of the woodcut and lithography was far more extensive among Art Nouveau artists than was the paint-box. Files of *The Studio,* mentioned earlier (and which began publication in 1893) , are a fertile source of artists' designs for creations ranging from furniture to wall hangings. Publications of kindred spirit in other countries are also valuable reference sources. These include *Pan,* founded in Berlin in 1895 and a staunch advocate of the *Jugendstil* movement; *Jugend,* established in Munich in 1896 and from whose name the German movement was derived; *Ver Sacrum,* started in Vienna in 1898; France's *L'Art Décoratif; The Chap-Book,* of Chicago; and various other periodicals devoted primarily to art and decoration which were established or flourished during the last decade of the nineteenth century.

Among the types of work that predominated in the field of the graphic arts were posters, book covers, title pages, page decorations, illustrations for articles and stories, bookplates, and lettering, some artists even designing new characters for type.

Charles Ricketts was one of the outstanding artists who decorated books, among them Oscar Wilde's *A House of Pomegranates,* and he made some striking contributions to book binding. Another book decorator was Otto Eckmann, who specialized in the floral version of *Jugendstil.* Many of his vignettes were published in *Pan.* The Norwegian Edvard Munch also worked in the *Jugendstil* mode, residing for some years in Berlin. He completed a number of outstanding paintings but also worked in the media of the woodcut, etching, and the lithograph. His work is characterized by the use of the sensuous curve that often imparts a seductive appeal.

In Vienna, Art Nouveau painting was spearheaded by Gustav Klimt, a master of ornament in its geometric versions, and outstanding among his works are his decorations painted for the University of Vienna's lecture auditorium.

The extraordinarily talented Henri van de Velde painted until he subsequently turned to such fields as the designing of furniture and accessories and graphic work, including posters. Ludwig von Hofmann not only was a painter but also an illustrator of books. The Dutch artist Toorop made fertile use of the whiplash line in his graphic work, and Ferdinand Hodler, the Swiss-German, developed a heavy type of Art Nouveau that was all his own, his achievements including a number of murals.

Undoubtedly, the outstanding artist in the United States whose work reflected the Art Nouveau spirit with remarkable success was William H. Bradley, so much of whose work, as mentioned above, was strongly influenced by Beardsley. A large number of Bradley's drawings appeared in *The Chap-Book*, of which he was editor from 1904 to 1905, and in other periodicals with which he was associated, including *Century Magazine*.

Bradley also executed numerous commercial posters for various businesses, including Victor Bicycle Company, and vignettes and covers for various periodicals, among these, interestingly, *The Inland Printer*, founded in Chicago in 1883 as a magazine of the printing trades and noted for its authoritative articles on the printing arts.

Bradley was a man of many talents. He designed type and founded the Wayside Press in Springfield, Massachusetts, and designed books and wrote several himself, including *Peter Poodle, The Wonderbox Stories, Spoils,* and *Lancelot and the Ladies*. Just as Beardsley influenced Bradley, so Bradley influenced several other American artists.

The poster today is a commercial art, and it may therefore

appear as something of a paradox that an aesthetic movement would tie itself so closely to commercialism. Yet, the father of the modern poster, Henri de Toulouse-Lautrec, was among the distinguished artists of his times (1864-1901). Toulouse-Lautrec is not considered an Art Nouveau painter; nevertheless, many of his theatrical posters reflect major elements of the Art Nouveau style, although they lack some of them, too, such as the floral motifs.

But the Art Nouveau poster did differ somewhat from the majority of posters whose prime emphasis was upon sales appeal; the emphasis in the former was upon art. In spite of this, the Art Nouveau poster flowered brilliantly not only abroad but also to a lesser extent in the United States during the waning years of the last century. The Japanese influence on the Art Nouveau style is reflected in some of the early posters of John Sloan, whose career started before he was out of his teens as a newspaper artist. But Sloan largely abandoned his early style.

Another American some of whose poster work bore close kinship to Art Nouveau was Frank Hazenflug, who did posters for *The Chap-Book* in the mid-1890's but about whose later work little appears to be known. In the Beardsley tradition was some of the work of Ethel Reed, of Boston, one of the very few women working in the poster medium in the late nineteenth century. The new style's influence was evident, too, in the posters of Louis Rhead, who came to the United States from England in the 1880's and who subsequently developed his own independent style which brought him renown as an illustrator. Like Bradley, Rhead also attained some success as an author, particularly for his *Robin Hood*. Other Americans who did at least some work under the new art's influence were E. B. Bird and Will Carqueville.

One most interesting aspect of poster art, which will help to explain its apparent paradox, was that despite the fact that the prime objective of the majority of posters was to help sell a product, a service, an event, or an idea, posters of merit have been sought from their beginnings as distinct contributions to art by *collectors*. Both artist and publisher looked for recompense not merely from their patron (client or customer, if you prefer) but also from the large numbers of collectors who avidly sought and paid well for outstanding posters.

· Producers of many posters, in fact, advertised them for sale. A large number were exhibited in galleries and were offered for sale by art dealers. Collectors' clubs were organized and functioned in much the same fashion as do those now focusing their attention upon the collecting of steins, bottles, music boxes, and dolls.

True, some of the Art Nouveau posters were intended to advertise products and commercial companies, but the majority were related to the promotion of such things as books, theatrical presentations, magazines, and calendars. Consequently, their artists were not confined by the necessity for the "hard sell." Moreover, excluding the billboard posters which are not within the scope of this discussion, nearly all pictorial posters were small enough to display in much the same manner as are paintings. This of course adds to the inducement for collecting them.

Now, once again, collectors are finding the art poster a prime attraction, and they are moving with alacrity in art galleries and the auction salesroom, a good many commanding prices of $50 to well over $100. Here indeed is a field in which the alert collector may profit if he is willing to search the byroads for examples that may be languishing in hideaways ranging from the attics of Victorian homes to the second floors of abandoned stores.

The renewal of their popularity is attested by the numerous reproductions that have lately put in their appearance—advertised and offered honestly as reproductions and intended to lend color and verve to the modern home, the office, and, not least, the college dormitory room. As collectors' items, these are valueless, but their originals seem quite likely to assume higher value, perhaps considerably higher, in the years ahead.

Already many fine posters have gravitated to museums and other institutions. At the Metropolitan Museum of Art in New York City, they will be found in the remarkable collections of the Print Department. The New York Public Library's Art Department also has a collection, and an increasing number of art museums are acquiring examples.

Books with Art Nouveau title pages, vignettes, initial letters, and other decorations have thus far been little sought and are available at most reasonable prices as is indicated in the final chapter of this book.

Sculpture was influenced little by the new style as compared with the fields we already have discussed. Among the few distinguished sculptors working in the mode, however, were Aristide Maillol of France, Georges Minne of Belgium, and Hermann Obrist of Germany. But Antonio Gaudí created for structures that he designed in Spain iron ornamentation in sculptural form that has never been surpassed, and he established for himself in Barcelona and indeed throughout Europe and Great Britain a reputation as one of the finest creative geniuses of the entire Art Nouveau movement. Similarly, in France Hector Guimard designed sculpture-like ornamentation for the striking Paris métro entrances that were the talk of the day and for years thereafter.

What sculpture was produced in the mood was intended chiefly as a part of the overall scheme of decoration in homes and other buildings.

The work of Maillol commands high respect today, particularly those sculptures created during that period in which he made such facile use of the sinuous line. This is the sculpture that virtually exudes *joie de vivre*—a term scarcely applicable to the work of Georges Minne, which is more akin in its near sepulchral aspects, if not in wickedness, to that of Aubrey Beardsley. In contrast to both Maillol and Minne, Obrist eschewed the human figure in his sculptures.

A darling of the sculptors—as well as of artists working in other medias—of the period was the American dancer Löie Fuller, who became a celebrity in Europe and whose long, shimmering veils at the apex of her dance were sent whirling upward and around in undulations that were of themselves a sort of fluid Art Nouveau. A sculptured likeness of her, showing the whirling veils, by Pierre Roche is preserved in the Musée des Arts Décoratifs in Paris as is another, kindred in spirit, by Raoul Larche, which was wired for a table lamp. Her fellow American Will Bradley captured her likeness in the graphic arts, his illustration entitled "Serpentine Dancer" having been published in *The Chap-Book*, and even Toulouse-Lautrec could not pass her by.

In the early twentieth century there appeared a variety of spelter castings of a dancing figure with these same swirling veils, almost unquestionably Löie Fuller, and these crop up in the antiques shops in England from time to time, mostly unsigned. They have been bringing only $20 to $30, recognized as to inspiration and acquired primarily for conversion into lamps.

Numerous other spelter or white metal castings in the Art Nouveau mode, many in vase form, were produced from the early 1900's until about the time of World War 1. These, too, have largely languished because they are not recognized as commercial Art Nouveau and may frequently be bought for quite small sums. The author recently purchased at auction a foot-tall vase form, whose top was formed of three fish heads with gulping mouths and for which he paid the grand total of $6.50. It is unidentified by markings but came from England, where it was presumably made.

Raoul Larche, incidentally, also did several other versions of Löie Fuller in bronze, and a few other sculptors of the same period created bronze dancers that seem almost surely to have been inspired by her, regardless of their models. Nude female figures with flowing draperies characterized numerous types of commercial decorative pieces ranging from wall plaques to clock cases. Other sculptured ornamental pieces in the Art Nouveau style were produced by Léo Laporte (Laporte-Blairsy), who also was a designer of jewelry, J. Causse, who specialized in the popular bronzes, Agathon Léonard, who created a series of Greek dancers that were originally made in bisque but metal-cast versions of which were made by the Susse Frères Foundry, and others.

The languid Art Nouveau female figure in diaphanous garments is also encountered frequently in lamp form or as candelabra, the figures providing the standard, and is incorporated in inkstands and ashtrays, as well.

Of Art Nouveau architecture we shall say nothing more, since, unless one purchases dwellings or other buildings, one does not collect architecture, only architectural elements.

XIV

What About Prices?

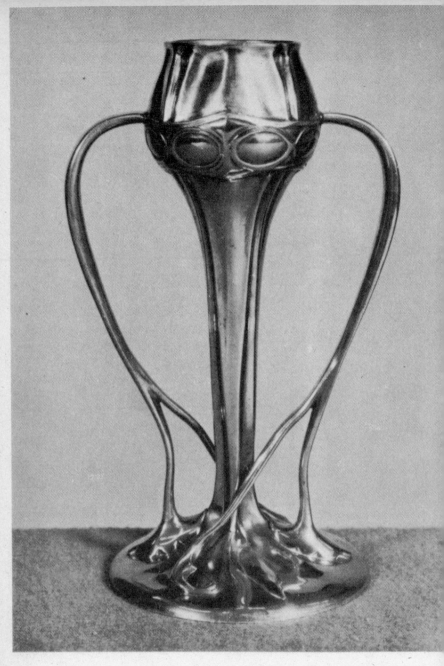

STRICTLY ART NOUVEAU IN FORM IS THIS PEWTER VASE BY IMBODY &
COMPANY, CA. 1903–4. *Courtesy, Victoria and Albert Museum, London.*

THE MONETARY VALUES of perhaps the majority of traditional antiques from earlier centuries are fairly well established. They may vary somewhat from one geographical area to another, but they remain within a fairly limited range, and knowledgeable dealers are well aware of them.

When it comes to the more recent collectible objects, including those in the Art Nouveau manner, however, it is a different story. Prices of comparable pieces of Art Nouveau glass tend to stay within a relatively narrow range, although they have tended to move upward rather sharply within the past few years. But generally there are really no established values for thousands of the newer types of Art Nouveau collectibles that are just being discovered or rediscovered, no matter what some dealer may tell you to the contrary.

Many Art Nouveau objects are lying around in shops catching dust because some shop proprietors, unaware of precisely what they are, relegated them to back rooms, storage boxes, and whatever nooks and crannies may not already be crammed with antiques. Therefore, customers do not always see them; and many of those who do have no more understanding of them than do their owners. It does appear likely that as more people become aware of what Art Nouveau is, these miscellaneous objects will be toted out of storage, dusted off, and their price tags raised.

Nevertheless, for awhile yet you may be able to find bargains galore in this intriguing field, and you are indeed likely to find prices on almost identical objects varying considerably from locality to locality and from shop to shop.

In this chapter we have compiled for your interest and information scores of prices that are being asked—as this is being written—for collectibles ranging from Art Nouveau glass to boudoir and costume accessories. These include prices at which certain articles have sold in recent months as well as those found on objects in numerous shops and those advertised currently in the various collector periodicals.

These are neither make-believe prices nor educated guesses as to what prices *should* be; they are the actual prices being asked by dealers, private and public, or received in shops and at auction. They were obtained by a study of recent auction records, visits to numerous antiques shops, and an exhaustive study of prices advertised by literally thousands of dealers. They are intended to serve merely as a guide to current asking prices, and it is conceivable that many of them may have changed, some perhaps drastically, by the time this book reaches your hands. We hope that these prices not only will be of interest to you but that they may be of special interest a few years hence. Should you decide to acquire Art Nouveau collectibles, they should help you determine after a few years whether you have invested wisely from a purely financial standpoint, although we hasten to add that it is our opinion that whoever invests in antiques from a financial standpoint only may not be the wisest of investors. Even so, it is a fact of life that antiques are now being acquired as never before as a hedge against the continuing inflationary pressures that seem to assault us with increasing frequency from cradle to grave.

As suggested earlier, perhaps the greatest monetary appreciation in the field of Art Nouveau has occurred lately in Tiffany glass; the magnificent early glass of Émile Gallé has not risen nearly so rapidly or so sharply.

A few prices brought by certain items of Tiffany glass were cited in the chapter on glass. It must be borne in mind that with Tiffany glass, as with all other individually handcrafted pieces, whether they be glass, pottery, or what not, the price should depend upon the quality of the individual piece itself, since no two will be precisely alike, even though they may appear quite similar. Price, consequently, will depend upon the skill of the dealer and the purchaser in detecting quality and the elements that make for desirability. Experience is the most important factor here in determining value.

Tiffany lamps and shades are in great demand, and prices of fine ones have soared within the past few years. One dealer recently advertised eight signed Tiffany lamps at prices of from $300 to $2,800 each. The same dealer offered "Tiffany-type" hanging lamps at $100 to $650 each. Collectors are willing to pay more for signed than unsigned pieces, and this is as good a time as any to emphasize that this very fact has resulted in a burgeoning business in forging signatures and that there are available for this nefarious but undoubtedly profitable undertaking kits to assist the unconscionable individual in this dishonest venture. And it cannot be repeated too often that if you do not know your glass, know your dealer.

Although it is of course difficult to visualize individual pieces of handcrafted work without actually seeing them, here are some prices of Tiffany glass with a brief description of each piece:

TIFFANY GLASS

Lamps

Bronze base with three iridescent gold (Favrile) shades, each numbered and signed L.C.T. and with base signed Tiffany Studios, 18 inches high overall, $800.

Acorn table lamp, 16 inches high, orange acorn with green leaded glass shade, $575.

Dragonfly lamp, $3,840 to $4,000.

Candlestick lamps with matching shades, one base mended, per pair, $600.

Bamboo lamp, signed, $7,000.

Desk lamp, brass base and bell-shaped standard with leaded green to blue bell-shaped shade, 20 inches high, $495.

Peony lamp, shade 22 inches in diameter with colored florals, leaves and sky, on bronze base, fully signed, $4,990.

Snail lamp, swirled bronze base with leaded glass snail shade, $595.

Iridescent yellow shade 10 inches in diameter signed L.C.T., Favrile, dome-shaped, on bronze base signed Tiffany Studios, $475.

Other Tiffany Glass

Paperweight vase, baluster-shaped, decorated with milky semiopaque white blossoms and green leafage on amber iridescent ground, signed L.C.T., Favrile 1927, 13¾ inches high and 4¾ inches at base, top warped in blowing (illustrated on page 219 of Robert Koch's *Louis C. Tiffany; Rebel in Glass*), $1,375.

Vase, 13 inches high, tapered, gold iridescent, tulip top, signed L.C. Tiffany, Favrile #8327-E, $285.

Vase, flower form, 8½ inches high, iridescent gold with green leaves and vines, signed and numbered, $395.

Vase, Lava glass, $3,500.

Vase, Cypriote, $1,650.

Vase, flower form, 4½ inches high, pastel turquoise flowers and opalescent stripes, 6-inch diameter, top opening, $400.

Vase, 6½ by 6 inches in diameter, Aquamarine, decorated with bubbly water with foam waterline and trailings of leaves and flowers, $2,500.

Vase, flower form, 8½ inches high, striped green leaf outlined in iridescent gold on each side, green leaves with adventurine on base, signed L.C.T., Favrile #991-V, $385.

Vase, stick type, 12¾ inches high, gold iridescent, signed L.C.T., Favrile, with metal base signed Tiffany Furnaces, Inc., $175.

Vase, 5 inches high, yellow with protruded chain and feather motif, signed, $570.

Bowl, 12 inches diameter, gold iridescent in concentric

circles of lime, pink, green, stretched edge top, signed L.C.T., Favrile #1561, $250.

Candlesticks, 8 inches high, blue Favrile glass stems, pair, $175.

Candlesticks, 4 inches high, pink iridescent, baluster stems with domed base, signed L.C.T., Favrile #1927, pair. $485.

Champagne glass, 6 inches high, opalescent pink with optic-ribbed molded bowl and green stem and base, signed L.C.T., Favrile, $335.

Champagne glass, 5 inches high, optic-ribbed green with turquoise ball on stem, signed L.C.T., $85.

Compote, 7 inches in diameter by 2½ inches high, iridescent gold, signed and with original paper label, $250.

Decanter, 12 inches high, intaglio cutting, iridescent gold, signed L.C. Tiffany, Favrile #306, $245.

Finger bowl and underplate, milliefiori-type design of flowers and leaves, both pieces signed L.C.T., $625.

Nut dish, 3 inches in diameter and 1½ inches high, blue iridescent, signed L.C.T. #A897, $69.50.

Toothpick holder, gold Favrile, pinched sides, $69.

Wine glass 7½ inches high, blue and white, $110.

The reader will, of course, have noted considerable price variations in some items of comparable shape and type.

GALLÉ GLASS

Cruet, enameled, ribbed amber with original stopper, enameled thistle in maroon, beige, and pink, applied handle, 7¾ inches high including stopper and 4½ inches in diameter at widest portion, made during Gallé's early period, $275.

Box, covered, cameo, deeply cut orange jonquils, kidney-shaped, $185.

Decanter, enameled, 1½ pints capacity, paneled ovoid body of pastel blue decorated with multicolored chrysanthemums, buds, and leaves, wafer base, 8 inches high and 4 inches at widest diameter, $360.

Goblet, enameled, amethyst, signed, $195.

Lamp (scent), cameo glass flacon in yellow with orange flowers and brown leaves and stems, metal collar and snuffer, used with both wick and perfume, $120.

Rose bowl, cameo, pale amethyst leaves and flowers against a frosted and pink ground, 2½ inches by 1½ inches across top, $85.

Vase, 12 inches high, four-layer cameo, four colors, carved clematis blossoms in amethyst with buds, leaves and vines in two tones of brown over orange to yellow matt-finish ground, pedestal foot, $375.

Vase, cameo, 6½ inches by 2½ inches widest diameter, trees and mountains, layers in purple, blue and clear, $205.

Vase, 4¾ inches high, cameo polished purple flowers on white acid ground, $120.

Vase, 14 inches high, cameo with tiger leaf design in dark and light brown, 6-inch-diameter base, $275.

Vase, cameo with carved nasturtiums, buds and leaves in gloss over frosty white matt ground, widest diameter 3¾ inches, $235.

Vase, 14 inches high, cameo with lavender and charcoal flowers and branches, tapering from 15½ inches at widest diameter to 3½-inch-diameter base, $250.

Vase, 7½ inches high, cameo, three layers, green leaves on pink and frosted ground, footed, $155.

Vase, 13 inchces high, cameo, forest scene in green and brown on apricot, white and green ground, $285.

Vase, 8 inches high, cameo, florals on pink, green, and brown ground, acid cut, $155.

Vase, 6⅝ inches high, cameo, banjo-shaped, green cut to lavender and white florals on frosted and salmon-pink ground, four acid cuttings, original retail store label, $135.

OTHER ART NOUVEAU GLASS

Daum Nancy

Bowl, cameo, 6 inches in diameter, floral, pink, green, and

violet, $189.

Box, cameo, 6 inches in diameter, covered, square with tapering sides, fuschia flowers, buds and leaves on white matt ground, $250.

Lamp, cameo, 11 inches high, lake scent at sunset, orange, pink, and yellow, $435.

Pitcher, cameo and enameled "Honesty" in tan against yellow, frost and green-spattered ground, 12 inches high, $275.

Rose bowl, cameo, rectangular, 4½ inches high, green leaves and red berries on frosted ground, $140.

Vase, cameo, 9 inches high, green, purple and orange florals on frosted ground, $125.

Vase, cameo, 8 inches high, cylindrical, maroon and gold branches, leaves and snail on frosted ground, $135.

Vase, cameo and enameled, 7 inches high, mistletoe berries on frosted ground with poem carved around base, $85.

Vase, cameo, 4 inches high, bowl-shaped, fruit in colors on gray, pink, and yellow matt ground, $225.

Tumbler, cameo, black and gold leaves and snails on blue ground, $100.

Delatte (Nancy, France)

Vase, cameo, 2½ inches high, dappled orange, bulbous, with definite Art Nouveau decor, $45.

Vase, cameo, 7¾ inches high, scenic with two acid cuttings, chartreuse, green, and brown on satin ground, $165.

Vase, cameo, 9¼ inches high, flattened ovoid body, branches, leaves, and pods in green and brown on pastel matt ground, $195.

Vase, cameo, 10½ inches high, three colors and four layers; elliptical and footed with florals on white matt ground, $135.

Durand

Bowl, footed, electric blue with silver vine and leaf tracery, $195.

Champagne, goblet, topaz with blue edges, $21.

Compote, 1½ inches high by 6¼ inches in diameter, blue with feather pattern, oval base, $157.50.

Plate, 8 inches in diameter, cranberry feather pattern, $160.

Vase, 6½ inches high, peacock blue, gold and pink highlights on iridescent apricot background, silver green dragloop design, $260.

Vase, 6½ inches high, green leaves and veining on orange iridescent base, $350.

Wine glass, cobalt with white feathering and vaseline foot and stem, $120.

Handel

Lamp, desk, 15 inches high, bronze base with 10-inch-long shade in green glass with bronze feather trim, $500.

Lamp, 23 inches high, pink shades 18 inches in diameter with handpainted birds, trees, and blossoms, three lights, artist-signed, $225.

Lamp, miniature, 7-inch-diameter shade with scenic view, bronze base, $125.

Shade, 17½ inches in diameter, chipped effect with yellow leaves, artist-signed, $55.

Shade, 14 inches high and 20½ inches in diameter, cream with handpainted leaves and tendrils, two lights, $100.

Vase, cream background with embossed scrolls around top and base, ribbed, with carnation and leaves, brass collar, signed, $65.

Imperial Art Glass

Bowl, 9 inches in diameter, purple leaf and vine decor, $125.

Creamer, rose, blue and gold iridescent with early mark, $47.50.

Vase, 7 inches high, opal base with green dragloopings, crackled orange inside finish, $175.

Vase, trumpet shape, 12½ inches high, purple leaf and vine decor, $110.

Kew Blas

Bowl, small, iridescent gold, $150.

Sherbet, iridescent gold, $115.

Tumbler, iridescent gold, signed, $150.

Vase, bulbous, pulled feather designs in green and brown on tan ground, footed, $590.

Vase, 11½ inches high, flask-shaped, gold iridescent with striped base, unsigned, $185.

Vase, 10 inches high, red iridescent over opal, decorated with gold and bronze, $195.

Lalique

Bird (sparrow), 5 inches long by 3½ inches high, $25.

Boat, cocoa brown trim on frosted background, $75.

Bottle, perfume, mushroom-shaped, pink with four iridescent gold floral panels, $25.

Box, covered, round, clear with milky opalscent beetles and vine in relief on lid, 6¾ inches in diameter, $55.

Dish, covered, 7 inches in diameter with lid covered by connecting scallops with small leaf designs on each, $75.

Cup and saucer, blue with embossed leaf designs, $39.50.

Bowl, 9½ inches in diameter, shell pattern, $65.

Bowl/vase, cire perdue, black enamel on sculptured frosted glass, 10½ inches high by 8 inches in diameter, $325.

Bowl, 12½ inches in diameter and 5½ inches high, molded mermaids and flowers, $250.

Fish, molded, 6½ inches long, open fins, signed in script, $40.

Goblet, 7½ inches high, nude figure stem, $20.

Jar, jam, 6 inches high, embossed butterflies all over, sterling silver lid, $40.

Lamp base, blue with bird and vine design, bulbous, 9 inches in diameter, $145.

Plate, blue lily pads molded on clear background, $40.

Plate, sandwich, 13½ inches in diameter, raised overlapping leaves, $60.

Pomade jar, 2½ inches high, fine ribbing, frosted daisies on lid (Houbigant), $24.

Toothpick holder, 3½ inches high, frosted, five nudes, $25.

Rose bowl, leaf and abstract florals, 6½ inches high, amber, $75.

Vase, 10x10 inches, lotus blossom, opalescent with raised petals, $150.

Vase, watermelon-shaped, 8¼ inches high, white with sunk flowers, $68.50.

Vase, bulbous, 6 inches at widest diameter, embossed leaves overlapping each other, $85.

Vase, 7 inches high, birds in relief, florals, frosty white, $135.

Vase, 9½ inches high, four birds in blue, $175.

Vase, 9½ inches high and 8 inches in diameter, frosted birds, $75.

La Verre Français

Chalice, cameo, 13 inches high, lavendar leaves, $135.

Ewer, cameo, 15 inches high, purple leaves on mottled cream ground, acid cutting, $150.

Lamp, cameo, mushroom-shaped, 21 inches high by 13 inches in diameter, $350.

Vase, cameo, 8½ inches high, orange and green leaves and seed pods on mottled yellow ground, $95.

Vase, cameo, 20 inches high, purple grapes, vines and leaves on rust ground, $300.

Vase, cameo, 8 inches high, brown florals on mottled camphor ground, $125.

Legras

Bowl, cameo, sauce-shaped, 8 x 5 x 3 inches high, leaves and berries, also enameled, $145.

Bowl, enameled, 2½ inches high and 9 inches in diameter, florals, $38.

Planter, enameled, 8½ inches wide by 3¼ inches high, orange and green decor, $98.

Vase, cameo, 9 inches high, foliage, maroon on frosted ground, $80.

Vase, enameled, 6 inches high, with Art Nouveau design

against satinized yellow-orange ground, $52.50.

Vase, enameled, 6 inches high, Art Nouveau design of butterflies and flowers in blue, black, and white against satinized orange-yellow ground, $60.

Vase, cameo, 10 inches high, trees and grass against pink sky; also enameled, $105.

Vase, cameo, 9 inches high, red maple leaves and stems on pink crackle ground, $135.

Loetz

Rose bowl, iridescent, egg-shaped on metal base decorated with figure of girl on each side, $125.

Vase, 3½ inches high and 6 inches wide, gold with blue iridescent pulled feather, $225.

Vase, 6¼ inches high, gold iridescent with red lily pads, $150.

Vase, 8½ inches high, blue iridescent, draped pattern with silver inlay floral-leaf design on front, pinched body, $150.

Vase, 6 inches high, peacock pattern with blue and gold, in metal holder, $85.

Muller Frères

Lamp, mushroom-shaped, frosted, shades of mottled orange, $125.

Lampshade, 6 inches high, pastel shades, $37.50.

Vase, cameo, 6 inches high, turquoise floral motif on turquoise and white ground, $185.

Vase, cameo, 13 inches high by 7 inches at widest diameter, forest scene in three shades on reddish-brown on orange, $475.

Vase, cameo, 5½ inches high, scenic in three shades of blue on cream, $345.

Vase, cameo, 5¾ inches high, scenic (signed Luneville), $130.

Nash

Bowl, chintz, 7½ inches at widest diameter by 1½ inches high, powdered green mottling between aquamarine stripes, signed Nash #409, $85.

Candlesticks, 12 inches high, chintz, pair, $195.

Centerpiece bowl, chintz, green with brown spirals, 12¾ inches at widest diameter, $185.

Plate, Cintra, signed, $85.

Phoenix

Vase, molded, 7 inches high, praying mantis, pink, $45.

Vase, molded, 7 inches high, trumpet vine, pink background, $35.

Vase, molded, 11 inches high, ivy and vines, brown background, $48.

Quezal

Bowl, 4½ inches in diameter with 5½-inch-diameter matching plate, calcite and gold, $325.

Bowl, 2½ x 2½ inches, gold iridescent, ribbed, lined in turquoise, $165.

Lamp, hanging, large, white with feather motif, including fixtures, $345.

Night light, 9¾ inches high, gold iridescent with brass base, $125.

Salt dish, ribbed, gold iridescent, $65.

Vase, small cabinet size, four-sided, flared top, gold iridescent, $160.

Vase, 8 inches high, autumn leaf with random threading, base drilled for lamp, $68.

Vase, 10 inches high, stick type, gold iridescent, $155.

Silver Deposit Glass

Celery dish, 5½ inches long, peacock and vine, $15.

Decanter, bulbous, with matching stopper, $15.

Pitcher, 9 inches high, flowers, buds and foliage, $45.

Sugar bowl, two handles, floral design in overlay, $8.50.

Whiskey set, five glasses and tray with thistles and leaves in overlay, $160 set.

Steuben

Biscuit jar, straight sides, gold, blue, and red, $235.

Bowl, 5 inches in diameter, vertical ribs, gold iridescent (Aurene), $165.

Bowl, console, 7 inches in diameter, gold Aurene on calcite, $85.

Compote, 7½ inches in diameter, gold Aurene, draped top with disc and ribbed bubble stem, original paper label, $250.

Cup and saucer, silver with gold Aurene lining, $90.

Tazza, 10½ inches high, gold Aurene, twisted stem, $370.

Vase, Jack-in-the-Pulpit type, 6½ inches high, gold Aurene, $250.

Vase, 6 inches high, stick type, blue Aurene, $110.

Vase, green leaf and vine decoration and paperweight flowers, signed "Aurene" and "Haviland," $225.

Vase, 3½ inches high, melon-shaped, gold Aurene, $125.

Vase, 10 inches high (acid cutback), jade green with butterfly wings and flowers carved in alabaster ground, $795.

Vase, 8 inches high (acid cutback), alabaster, fan-shaped and footed, carved flowers and leaves, $450.

Webb (Thomas and Sons)

Biscuit jar, cameo, 5 inches in diameter and 3 inches high, intaglio cut florals, cranberry, $85.

Pitcher, 8 inches high, cased glass of red with white lining, enameled florals and butterfly, $250.

Perfume bottle, cameo, 3¾ inches high, red under white, violets, buds, and leaves, $350.

Perfume bottle, cameo, lying-down type, 6½ inches long, citrus with white flowers, $200.

Vase, cameo, 7½ inches high, amphora-shaped, poppies, buds, leaves and butterflies, $800.

ART NOUVEAU POTTERY AND PORCELAIN

Prices of Art Nouveau pottery and porcelain appear on the rise, and this is particularly true of certain patterns in Weller, Roseville, Rookwood, and other pottery. Some choice pieces of Van Briggle pottery remain at low prices and could prove a good investment.

Gallé

Bowl, swan-shaped, 8½ x 7 inches, enameled decorations, signed E. Gallé, Nancy, $175.

Compote, footed, 9 x 4½ inches, decorated with guardsman in center, $125.

Creamer, 5½ inches high, owl design, $175.

Cup and saucer, faience, cup 4⅜ inches in diameter, floral and scenic decorations, $150.

Jug, 7¼ inches high, handled, floral, brown glaze, $185.

Buffalo Pottery

Candlesticks, Emerald Deldare, pair, $175.

Gloriana pitcher, 9½ inches high, multicolor decoration on blue, figural and scenic, $115.

Jug, marine scenic, 9 inches high and 5¾ inches at widest diameter, $94.50.

Plate, 7¼ inches in diameter, Dr. Syntax series, $100.

Pitcher, 6 inches high, Dr. Syntax series, $150.

Tobacco humidor, 7 inches high, Dr. Syntax series, chip, $200.

Tray, calling card, Dr. Syntax series, $125.

Owens Pottery

Bowl, pastel high glaze, reverse shading blue-gray to gray-white with dragonfly, signed L. Lassel, $75.

Match holder, 2⅜ inches high, yellow, orange, and green floral and leaf decor, $32.

Pitcher, tankard, 12½ inches high, orange tulips and green leaves on brown to green ground, $43.

Vase, 10½ inches high, bottle-shaped, glossy glaze, wild orchid decor, $95.

Rookwood

Cream pitcher and sugar bowl, standard glaze, 1893, showing Japanese influence, set $350.

Ewer, 10 inches high, floral, buds and leaves on brown and yellow ground, 1898, signed by Lenore Asbury, $230.

Ewer, 6½ inches high, floral and leaves, 1899, signed by Edith Felton, $165.

Jug, handled, cherries and leaves, 1898, signed by Lenore Asbury, $165.

Stamp box, floral decor, artist-signed, 1894, $80.

Tea set (teapot, creamer, and covered sugar), glossy with butterfly handles, 1893, signed by Amelia Sprague, $425.

Vase, 6 x 6 inches, yellowish berries and leaves, green handle, notched lip, 1893, signed by Amelia Sprague, $150.

Vase, 7¼ inches high, Iris glaze, floral on green ground, signed C.A.B., $120.

Roseville Pottery

Ewer, 6 inches high, handled, brown and green, high glaze with wheat design, Rozane, $65.

Tobacco jar, high glaze, signed Dunlevy, pictorial, Rozane, $95.

Vase, yellow-olive to green-olive, burnt orange floral spray, signed P. Myers, Rozane Royal, $62.50.

Vase, 9 inches high, floral, initialed H.A.W., ca. 1900, Rozane, $45.

Vase, 7½ inches high, clover decor, Rozane, $30.

Vase, 8½ inches high, stick-type, yellow floral and green leaves and brown glaze, Rozane, $39.50.

Royal Doulton

Candlesticks, Kyle pattern of green shamrocks and yellow hearts, 6½ inches high, pair, $16.50.

Candlesticks, 9½ inches high, Art Nouveau decor in beige and brown, pair $82.50.

Pitcher, 8½ inches high, impressed leaves in brown on mottled green-brown ground, initialed by artist, $47.50.

Vase, 4½ inches high, and 3½ inches in diameter, sterling overlay in Art Nouveau flowers, Flambé, $75.

Vase, 13 inches high, veined, Flambé, $115.

Vase, 6¼ inches high, woodland scene, Flambé, $48.

Vase, 4¼ inches high, veined, Flambé, $46.

Tiffany Pottery

Bowl, 2½ inches in diameter, unglazed, floral decor on textured background, $65.

Bowl, bronze overlay, low floral relief, impressed L.C.T. monogram, F.P. #150, $285.

Planter, bowl shape, 15 inches in diameter and 9 inches high, raised flowers, yellow glaze, $180.

Vase, 7¼ inches high, shades of green in leaf shapes, signed L.C.T., $225.

Van Briggle Pottery

Bowl vase, blue with huge dragonflies, plus a flower holder with three frogs, two pieces, each signed, $49.50.

Bowl, 5 inches high and 7¾ inches in diameter, stylized flowers in blended turquoise, $28.

Lamp, small, blue with butterfly shade, $20.

Vase, 5½ inches high by 2¾ inches in diameter, floral, $10.50.

Vase, 8½ inches high, floral relief design on maroon, $15.

Vase, 10 inches high, lily decor, signed, $12.50.

Vase, 7½ inches high, bud forms in blue to green, ca. 1903, $20.

Vase, 7 inches high, dragonflies, purple ground, $20.

Weller

Aurelian pattern vase, bulbous, 6 inches high, floral, artist-signed, $38.

Aurelian vase, 13 inches high, foliage and berries on black background, $50.

Aurelian vase, 12½ inches high, floral, artist-initialed, $55.

Louwelsa pattern ewer, 4½ inches high, leaves, berries, trefoil spout, $28.

Louwelsa jug, 6½ inches high, floral on dark brown, artist-initialed, $45.

Louwelsa jardiniere with stand, 23½ inches high, floral, $65.

Louwelsa vase, drooping poppy, bud and pod, mustard-yellow to dark brown, signed C. Minnie Terry, $62.50.

Louwelsa vase, pillow-shaped, 7½ x 8 inches, acorns and leaves, $72.50.

Louwelsa vase, 11¾ inches high, yellow florals with green stems and leaves, glossy brown glaze, $42.50.

Sicardo pattern bowl, 5 inches high and 5½ inches in diameter, iridescent maroon, blues and greens with Art Nouveau florals, $150.

Sicardo vase, 5½ inches high, gourd-shaped, green and gold stylized flowers and leaves on pink-purple ground, $135.

Sicardo vase, 13½ inches high, thistles, $165.

Vase, no pattern named, 12 inches high, Art Nouveau decor, matt finish, $55.

Tankard, no pattern named, 13½ inches high, decorated with female figure in sheer garment, flowers and leaves, shades of pink and green, matt finish, $75.

Vase, no pattern named, 13 inches high, Art Nouveau form, red flowers on gray background shading to white, $45.

As mentioned earlier, various other potteries produced a number of pieces in Art Nouveau shapes or with Art Nouveau decoration. A few prices of miscellaneous pieces may be of interest. Gathering momentum among collectors is Teplitz ware, a good bit of which was made around the turn of the century in Austria. Many pieces were exported to the United States and sold in gift shops and even five-and-ten-cent stores. Now prices are on the rise. A Teplitz vase in Art Nouveau style, 15 inches high and picturing lavendar trees against a blue sky, a red rose against a green background at bottom, and a center of dragonflies is offered at $95. Six months earlier the same vase had been tendered at $75. Another Teplitz vase just 4½ inches high and featuring dragonflies on a green background has a price tag of $55.

A very late nineteenth-century Sèvres vase, 12½ inches tall, with peacock coloring and ormolu-mounted handles, featuring Art Nouveau clusters of grapes and leaves extending downward from the rim, is priced at $110.

The Royal Bayreuth factory (not located at Bayreuth at all but several miles away in Tettau, Germany) numbered among its quite numerous designs and patterns a good many pieces in the Art Nouveau style. A tray showing in relief a lithe woman with flowing hair and clothed in a flowing and diaphanous garment is priced at just $40. The tray measures 7 x 10 inches.

In the United States, Pickard, Inc., now located in Antioch, Illinois, and specializing still—as it has since its beginning— in hand decorated china, did a few pieces around the turn of this century in the Art Nouveau manner. Such a vase with stylized flowers in silver with gold tips has an asking price of $45. A Cambridge Art Pottery vase $9\frac{1}{2}$ inches high with orange and yellow berries on thorny stems and green and rust leaves is priced at $39.

An unsigned kidney-shaped box designated as unmarked R. S. Prussia china and featuring a female head in high relief surrounded by flower petals bears a $50 price. An unidentified ceramic plate marked only "Art Nouveau" and done in predominantly green and yellow colors is tendered at $11, and an Art Nouveau pitcher featuring thistles and leaves and marked only "J.H.A., Germany" is priced at $22.50.

ART NOUVEAU JEWELRY

What prices Art Nouveau jewelry may bring at auction can be answered only with educated guesses, since not a great amount of it has appeared in the salesrooms. A striking brooch created by René Lalique brought more than $1,400 in London a couple of years ago—but that piece incorporated diamonds, which have an inherent value, whereas many articles of Art Nouveau jewelry were fashioned of far less expensive materials. Another Lalique creation, a tiara set with diamonds, brought $700, and a record for jewelry in this mode was established in 1969 with the sale for $7,200 of a pendant created at the turn of the century for Philip Wolfers.

Certain other Lalique pieces have brought considerable sums, including $4,320 paid for a gold-and-sapphire ring in the shape of one of this artisan's famous nudes and an enameled gold-and-opal pendant sold for more than $1,200.

On the other hand, numerous items of jewelry made by lesser hands and of lesser materials have sold recently for quite small sums, and thousands of others are still available at prices of under $50. Even more objects are available in the trinket category for just a few dollars each. Moreover, one can still find some of the work of Lalique available from shops and from private sellers at low sums: witness a Lalique jewel box with paneled classical figures adorning it in relief and measuring 5 inches in diameter by 3½ in height recently advertised for only $32! True, the box had a few minor chips inside the cover, but it bore the renowned Lalique signature. Perhaps this was a "sleeper," but it also must be remembered that the house of Lalique is still being operated by the master's son. In addition, by no means all dealers in such wares are as yet "hip" to Art Nouveau and its resurgence in popularity.

Here are some recent prices asked for or brought by jewelry and trinkets in the Art Nouveau mode:

Pin, 1⅜ inches long, with two large opals, five pearls, and two-pronged mounted diamonds, $450.

Gold watch pin, $27.50.

Silver barrette, $25.

Gold locket, medium size, $75.

Gold-filled bracelet with locket on top, $35.

Gold lapel pin with enameled pink flower, green leaf, and pearl in flower's center, $27.50.

Buckle featuring scarabs and a jeweled Egyptian-type motif, $35.

Chain and picture locket with two compartments, $8.50.

Bronze Medusa-type heads mounted as cuff links, pair, $15.

Gold dragonfly pin with olivine eyes and two rubies in the body, $150.

ART NOUVEAU SILVER

As is the case with jewelry, many Art Nouveau silver pieces will have their prices tied to a large extent to the inherent value of the silver whereas silver-plated articles often go for a song. It should be borne in mind that these plated articles whose coating of silver has been worn can be replated and restored to their original pristine beauty—at a price, and sometimes a stiff one.

For your guidance, here are recent prices of miscellaneous sterling silver objects, and you will find scores of others listed in the advertising columns of the collector periodicals:

Gorham water pitcher with floral motifs, $300.

Unger Brothers shaving mug with Indian Chief head, $95.

Bread tray, 15 inches long, with pierced handles and floral motif, $225.

Embossed liquor flask, 6 inches high, monogrammed, $55.

Shoehorn, sterling handle depicting female with flowing hair, $10.

Cigar cutter with the familiar lady with flowing hair, $10.

Letter opener, 4 inches long, with female Art Nouveau figure in relief and open work, $5.25.

Three-branched candelabra, plated, signed Jarvie, $45.

Toothpick holder with butterflies on lily pad, plated, $11.

Sterling souvenir spoons with Art Nouveau motifs are still relatively plentiful at prices ranging from around $5 to $15. There are several dealers who specialize in inactive silver patterns, and those interested in Art Nouveau tablewares might find it profitable to check their advertisements or their stocks carefully for pattern names given in the chapter on silver.

"White metal" clocks with Art Nouveau figures have sold in shops recently at prices of $35 to $75 or so, but we have

witnessed the sale of quite a number of them in recent
months at auctions for dealers only at prices of under $40.
They were produced during the commercial period of the
movement and some verge on monstrosity. Watches will depend for their value on whether their cases are gold, gold-
filled, or silver and on the quality of their movements and
will range from under $50 to several hundred dollars. Watch
fobs will bring $3 to $20, most of them under $10.

As for that broad field encompassing articles of special interest to women, there are a host of boudoir and costume
accessories available for a few dollars each in commercial
versions of Art Nouveau. Articles of sterling silver or gold
come higher of course. Here are some miscellaneous prices
that should be of interest:

Ten-piece sterling dresser set by Unger Brothers, including
mirror, hairbrush, whisk broom, clothes brushes, wax cutter,
and manicure items, with female figure with flowing tresses
decorating each, $90.

Sterling hairbrush, 8¾ inches long, Cupid center motif,
$55.

Sterling hairbrush with handle in form of a woman's body,
9¾ inches long, $85.

Powder jar with silver-plated top decorated with head
with flowing hair, $20.

Sterling mirror and brush set, $22.

Sterling button hook, $4.50.

Hand mirror, $12.50.

Dress pin decorated with floral cones, $4.50.

Ceramic hatpin holder of Willets Belleek with cloud effect
and relief decoration, $20.

Alligator handbag with silver frame created of flowing
lines and featuring languid female with flowing gown and
hair, $45.

Hatpin with porcelain knob and medallion with flowers,
$15.

Hatpin holder, ceramic, stylized flowers, Austrian, $9.

Plated card holder on standard 6 inches high with stylized floral decoration on top, resilvered, $39.50.

Articles of a somewhat similar nature but with their primary appeal to men will fall within a similar price range. A sterling military brush, 7¼ inches long, decorated with a female head with flowing hair, is priced at $7.50, which is probably low. A cast iron ashtray adorned with a similar figure in its well is offered at $8. It was originally an advertising piece intended to promote Franroy cigars. A heavy brass pipe rack featuring a woman's profile and with a capacity of six pipes is offered at $31 and a brass paperclip in peacock form at $14. An Art Nouveau sterling cigar cutter (differing from the one listed above) has an asking price of $35. Ceramic tobacco jars will bring between about $25 and $50, and match safes will range between $5 and $25, depending on the material of which they are made—those of sterling usually obtaining the higher prices.

Writing accessories, except for inkstands and bottles, have not been widely collected, so firm values are not established for many categories of these. A brass stamp box marked Tiffany Studios was advertised for sale at $38. Inkstands depend for their price on the materials of which they are made and the quality of the workmanship that went into them. You'll find them ranging from around $10 up—the better ones in sterling and brass considerably up. Penholders have been almost totally ignored thus far, so they can probably be acquired for very little indeed, perhaps a dollar or so, and the same goes for fountain pens. Brass letter openers may be found for $10 or less, but silver ones can cost up to around $40 or $50 and some of bronze will bring above $10—some almost as much as those of silver.

Fruit bowls or brides' baskets of Art Nouveau-decorated glass in silver-plated stands or holders are priced in a wide range that extends from $50 to $250. You must judge these according to their quality, the type of glass, and the condition of the silver plate. Cruet or caster sets with bottles have been selling at $30 to $50, with the exception of those with cut bottles which often bring more. Salt and pepper shakers will range from a couple of dollars to $10 or more. A copper coffee set with a 14½ x 12-inch tray, a sugar bowl and a creamer, all featuring Art Nouveau floral decor, is priced at $42.50.

Other miscellaneous Art Nouveau prices of late have included the following:

Picture frame, brass, 14 x 17 inches, easel back, with reclining female figure on top and winged cherub at base, $22.

Brass door knocker, 4 x 3 inches, in form of woman's head with flowers in her hair, $10.

Copper and brass bookends with embossed decoration of stylized flowers, 5¾ inches high, pair, $38.

Thermometer, 9¾ inches high, with bronze half-form female figure, $15.

Book rack decorated with female heads with flowing hair, $15.

Candleholder, 7 inches high, with adjunct of reclining female figure in bronze finish, $12.

Art Nouveau "Fileuse" French lamp with bronzed figure of woman, $75.

Gilt-bronze lamp in form of the dancer Löie Fuller, signed by Raoul Larche, $1,344.

Art Nouveau student lamp in bronze with two signed Steuben shades of Ivorine with green and gold iridescent feather motif, 24 inches high and with sockets, dated 1909, $180.

Bronze centerpiece bowl with mottled green enamel and grape cluster handles, signed Carl Sorensen, $30.

Pewter plate, 8½ inches in diameter, with relief figure of woman with flowing locks, $25.

Bronze Art Nouveau footed plate, 9½ inches in diameter, $60.

Bronze vase with relief insects and florals, signed Moreau, $35.

Because so comparatively few pieces of Art Nouveau furniture have come on the market, prices for this category are also exceedingly difficult to establish. Most fine pieces of the early period are now in museums or private collections, but some do occasionally appear on the market. Not long ago, an intriguing inlaid table by Émile Gallé was offered by an antiques dealer for $275. This may seem a rare bargain a few years hence. Other sales within the past year or so have included an étagère, carved and painted by Louis Majorelle, for almost $600 and a small Mackintosh center table for slightly more than $600. It appears virtually certain at this time that future offerings of furniture by recognized Art Nouveau master craftsmen and designers will fetch substantial sums.

Hundreds of books with Art Nouveau title pages and decorations remain available at low prices, although those with special bindings will bring much more. The task of the collector who seeks such books is to search the shelves and boxes of the rare and out-of-print book shops for volumes with names of illustrators that he recognizes or with title pages and decorations that are obviously Art Nouveau in manner. This can be time-consuming, but it also can be a delightful chore. A simpler way is to obtain as many catalogues as you can from the out-of-print book shops, many of which issue such catalogues at intervals, some several times annually. There is no charge for the majority of these, although if you fail to place an order during the course of about a year, you may find your name removed from the mailing list.

Works of art, including paintings and sculptures, by artists who worked in the Art Nouveau style do appear more frequently at auction and in shops. A few recent prices include the following:

Painting by Kadinsky, *Rapallo—Boot im Meer,* 9¼ x 13 inches, $26,000.

Lithograph by Alphonse Mucha, *Le Petit Job,* framed 20¼ x 15¼ inches, $750.

Lithograph by Mucha, *Le Grand Job,* 40 x 60 inches, $700.

Lithograph by Mucha, *Monac-Monte Cerlo,* 28 x 42 inches, $575.

Signed Kaube Art Nouveau bronze figure on vase, 5¼ inches high, $175.

Bronze by Maillol, *La Méditerranée,* 6¼ inches high, $12,000.

Bronze by Maillol, *Leda,* 11½ inches high, 1900, $16,000.

Art Nouveau female figure, 4 inches high, untitled and by unidentified sculptor, $40.

A poster calendar for 1897 done by Edward Penfield, sold for $130, and other Penfield posters have been sold at prices of from $50 to $70. Louis Rhead posters have been priced as high as $250. Other posters in the style by known artists will fall between around $50 and $200.

The best way to acquire any sort of Art Nouveau at reasonable prices right now is to familiarize yourself as thoroughly as possible with the various characteristics of the style and with the names of the artists, designers, and craftsmen who created these objects. No matter what the experts tell you, it is still possible to discover "sleepers"—and this is indeed a great feeling!

XV

On the Trail of the Prize

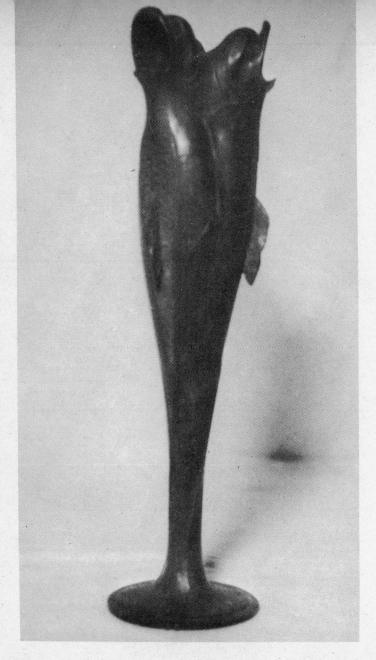

THIS BRONZE VASE IS CHARACTERIZED BY THE MERGED BODIES OF THREE FISH (THE THIRD CANNOT BE SEEN IN THE PHOTOGRAPH). IT WAS MADE IN ENGLAND BY AN UNIDENTIFIED PRODUCER. *Author's collection.*

HAVING CONSIDERED THE BACKGROUND of Art Nouveau, when and where objects in the style were created, and something about values, the question that will arise in many readers' minds is just where indeed one may hope to encounter an array of these pieces for the sport of purchasing.

One may, if he wishes and has sufficient funds to spare, visit the metropolitan auctions and bid on the scarce objects offered there. These are not likely to become his for a pittance, because, to date at least, the major auction houses have offered little in the way of commercial Art Nouveau, but instead have concentrated upon offerings of major objects with which the names of distinguished designers or fabricators are associated. We have discussed some of the prices that these pieces—Tiffany glass, Mackintosh furniture, work by Lalique and Gallé and others of the period—have brought. If a collector is sufficiently well-heeled, he may, to be sure, make acquisitions at these sales that will prove a good investment from the financial standpoint, but unless he has plenty of ready cash, he is not likely to be able to make too many major purchases. The dealer is in a different category: he buys and sells. Therefore, he may recoup his investment in short order, although this is not invariably true.

The average collector who would like to acquire as many examples as possible in the Art Nouveau style might be better advised to turn elsewhere and to concentrate on objects that are not unique, which is not to say that he should completely shun the metropolitan auctions; these are both enjoyable and educational, and even today bargains may be encountered at any auction, large or small. But it is the small-town auction that is more likely to offer the commercial versions of these treasures. Sometimes they may go for a pittance because they are not yet recognized for what they are.

However, do not make the mistake of underestimating the astuteness of the small-town auctioneer. In these days when the population explosion continues to push city boundaries ever outward, there is really no longer any such thing as a country bumpkin. And if you have had dealings of late with those you thought were bumpkins from the hinterlands, the chances are that you have found yourself out-slickered. The small-town auctioneer may indulge in the tobacco-auction chant which is still largely unintelligible to many of us city folk, but he knows a cachepot from a cachet, which is more than some collectors do.

Even so, since so many of these commercial Art Nouveau pieces are still unfamiliar to dealers and collectors alike, there is always the possibility that they will be offered at auctions in the smaller communities, unrecognized not only by the auctioneer but also by most of his audience. These will be, the chances are, pieces that have been acquired with the purchase of the entire contents of homes. Those in the audience may bid spiritedly for a Lalique perfume bottle or a Deldare plate, but silence may engulf them when an Art Nouveau figurine is tendered or a Van Briggle pottery vase is pulled forth from a box bulging with bric-a-brac and what the elite call bijouterie.

Once upon a time the country auction was the place where city slickers went for bargains, but no longer. I have attended many of them during recent years in the hope of snatching a few genuine bargains from under the noses of my fellows, including my elders and betters; and many of my acquaintances from the cities who have followed suit will confirm my finding that country bargains today are as rare as laying hens in penthouses. Still, just as the city auctions are, they are fun to attend and they, too, can provide an education in values of what is being bought and sold in the antiques market place today.

Large quantities of commercial Art Nouveau miscellany were produced in England, and an ever-increasing number of American antiques dealers are now purchasing heavily from English wholesalers. Many of these place orders for containers full of goods to be shipped to them and give the wholesalers carte blanche to fill up the nooks and crannies of these containers with small objects of the latters' choosing. Often the hollow interiors of grandfather clock cases are stuffed with small objects, since size rather than weight is the cost factor in sea shipments. Often small Art Nouveau objects are utilized to fill the empty spaces.

The author has recently encountered in a number of wholesale and retail antiques establishments in this country large numbers of such things as small Art Nouveau spelter figures and small Art Nouveau pottery vases that have come from both England and France and that have been priced quite inexpensively. There is a wholesale antiques establishment in Atlanta, Georgia—Atlanta Wholesale Antiques—that holds regular auctions for dealers and decorators only. Many cast spelter Art Nouveau style figurines have been offered there in recent months and have fetched only $10 to $20 each. Converted into lamps, which is just what many dealers do with them, these figures bring three to four times those amounts. This particular establishment offered not long ago a figure identified by the auctioneer as a rendition of Löie Fuller, which indeed it was; but no one in the audience on that occasion had heard of the darling of Art Nouveau artists, and not a bid was offered. It still languishes in the storeroom but will not for long, because your author fully intends to carry it home with him before the week is out.

The showrooms of many of these wholesalers who are making substantial purchases of antiques and collectibles from England and the Continent currently abound in miscellaneous pieces of Art Nouveau—Minton ceramics, Teplitz and Royal Dux vases and figures, European glass in the Art Nouveau mood, and so on. Since admission to and purchase from wholesalers is limited to legitimate dealers, the average collector does not ordinarily have access to these showrooms. However, the majority of collectors are on excellent terms with one or more retail dealers in their communities. If your relationship with a dealer is friendly enough (which sometimes means if you have made enough purchases from him), he may very well be induced to purchase what you want from the wholesalers and sell it to you at a smaller markup than is customary with him, since he knows he has an immediate sale.

Naturally, you would want to see what is available before placing an order. Many wholesalers will permit their dealer friends to bring their customers into their showrooms to select items they desire. You can't make the purchase direct but your dealer can. Wholesalers who permit dealers to bring in customers to select goods usually have their merchandise priced in code, so you are not likely to determine the wholesale prices anyway unless your dealer is willing to tell you what he paid for what you want.

Don't neglect the antiques shows in the small and medium-sized communities. They often attract small dealers from over a wide area, and not infrequently they will bring with them for display and sale small Art Nouveau pieces with which they are not familiar themselves but with which you should be. Don't expect to find bargains at the smaller shows in Quezal or Kew Blas vases or Lalique's molded glass, because so much has been written in the past two or three years about this glass that there are few dealers unfamiliar with it. Try, instead, looking about for miscellaneous pottery and porcelain (aside from Rookwood, Weller, Roseville, and Buffalo pieces, which have lately been in the spotlight), small items of jewelry, boudoir accessories, smoking sets, and any of the other considerable variety of things which we have considered and which have not yet been the subject of books and magazine articles.

Private house sales always hold possibilities, but bear in mind what we said earlier about such purported sales conducted by professionals. The best possibilities are auctions held on private premises at the dispersal of estates, particularly small ones. Try to get there early and look over in advance what is coming up for sale.

Finally, try to read the advertisements in one or more of the collector periodicals regularly. Art Nouveau collectibles are cropping up increasingly in these ads and often at prices that seem quite low. For the impecunious collector, one of the following periodicals may offer the best opportunities, and their addresses are listed in case you want to write for a sample copy of any with which you are not acquainted:

The Antiques Journal, P.O. Box 1050, Dubuque, Iowa 52001; *Spinning Wheel,* Exchange Place, Hanover, Pennsylvania 17331; *Hobbies,* 1006 South Michigan Avenue, Chicago, Illinois 60605; *Western Collector,* 511 Harrison, San Francisco, California 94105; *National Antiques Review,* Box 619, Portland, Maine 04014; and *Collector's Weekly,* P.O. Box 1119, Kermit, Texas 79745. There also are several others and, of course, there is the magazine *Antiques,* 551 Fifth Avenue, New York, New York 10017, which concerns itself primarily with the traditional antiques and is full of authoritative information about them.

Should you want to keep in touch with values, you can purchase one or more of the several antiques price guides that are now available and all of which are helpful. These are usually updated at regular intervals, and although they have not so far focused much attention on the field of Art Nouveau, it is likely that they soon will, because their compilers keep abreast of the collectible objects that are in demand and try to include typical prices. Price guides should never be used to set values, but they can serve as helpful aids in determining current selling prices around the country.

These guides include the following: *The Antique Trader Price Guide to Antiques & Collectors' Items,* by the author of the book you are now reading; *The Complete Antiques Price List,* by Ralph and Terry Kovel; *Warman's Antiques and Their Current Prices,* by E. G. Warman, and *Official Guide to Popular Antiques, Curios: the Price to Buy & Sell,* by Hal L. Cohen.

Selected Bibliography for Further Reading

Altman, Seymour and Violet, *The Book of Buffalo Pottery*. New York, Crown Publishers, Inc., 1969.

Barilli, Renato, *Art Nouveau*. London and New York, Paul Hamlyn, 1969.

Battersby, Martin, *Art Nouveau*. London and New York, Paul Hamlyn, 1969.

———, *The World of Art Nouveau*. New York, Funk & Wagnalls, 1969.

Beardsley, Aubrey, *The Early Work of Aubrey Beardsley* and *The Later Work of Aubrey Beardsley*. New York, Dover Publications, Inc., 1967.

Blount, Berniece and Henry, *French Cameo Glass*. Des Moines, Iowa, Privately published, 1968.

Bogue, Dorothy McGraw, *The Van Briggle Story*. Colorado Springs, Colorado, Privately published, 1968.

Davis, Derek C. and Middlemas, Keith, *Colored Glass*. New York, Clarkson N. Potter Inc., Publisher, 1968.

Deknatel, Frederick B., *Edvard Munch*. New York, The Museum of Modern Art, 1950.

Ericson, Eric E., *A Guide to Colored Steuben Glass, 1903–1933*. Denver, Colorado, Privately published, 1963.

Freeman, Dr. Larry, comp. *Victorian Posters*. Watkins Glen, New York, The American Life Foundation, 1969.

Freer Gallery of Art, *The Whistler Peacock Room*. Washington, D.C., The Freer Gallery of Art of the Smithsonian Institution, 1951.

Gillon, Edmund V., Jr., comp., *Art Nouveau: an Anthology of Design and Illustration from The Studio.* New York, Dover Publications, 1969.

Grover, Ray and Lee, *Art Glass Nouveau.* Rutland, Vermont, Charles E. Tuttle Company, 1967.

Hutter, Heribert, *Art Nouveau,* trans. by J.R. Foster. New York, Crown Publishers, Inc., 1967.

Jervis, Simon, *Victorian Furniture.* London, Ward Lock & Co. Limited, 1968.

Koch, Robert, *Louis C. Tiffany: Rebel in Glass.* New York, Crown Publishers, Inc., 1964.

Lee, Ruth Webb, *Nineteenth Century Art Glass.* New York, M. Barrows & Company, Inc., 1962.

Lichten, Frances, *Decorative Art of Victoria's Era.* New York, Charles Scribner's Sons, 1950.

Madsden, Stephan Tschudi, *Sources of Art Nouveau.* New York, George Wittenborn, 1955.

McClinton, Katharine Morrison, *Collecting American Nineteenth Century Silver.* New York, Charles Scribner's Sons, 1968.

Morrison, Hugh, *Louis Sullivan, Prophet of Modern Architecture.* Gloucester, Massachusetts, Peter Smith, Publisher, 1958.

Peck, Herbert, *The Book of Rookwood Pottery,* New York, Crown Publishers, Inc., 1968.

Pellicer, A. Cirici, *1900 en Barcelona: Modernismo, Modern Style, Art Nouveau, Jugendstil.* Barcelona, Spain, Ediciones Poligrafa, distributed by Tudor Publishing Company, New York.

Pevsner, Nikolaus, *Pioneers of Modern Design from William Morris to Walter Gropius,* revised ed. New York, The Museum of Modern Art, 1958, distributed by Doubleday & Company, Inc., Garden City, New York.

———, *The Sources of Modern Architecture and Design.* New York, Frederick A. Praeger, Publishers, 1968.

Porucho, Juan, *Gaudi: an Architect of Anticipation.* Barcelona, Spain, Ediciones Poligrafa, 1968, distributed by Tudor Publishing Company, New York.

Purviance, Louise and Evan, and Schneider, Norris F., *Zanesville Art Pottery in Color*. Leon, Iowa, Mid-America Book Company, 1968.

Rainwater, Dorothy T. and Felger, Donna H., *American Spoons*. Camden, New Jersey, Thomas Nelson & Sons and Everybodys Press, 1969.

Revi, Albert Christian, *American Art Nouveau Glass*. Camden, New Jersey, Thomas Nelson & Sons, 1968.

———, *Nineteenth Century Glass: its Genesis and Development*, rev. ed. Camden, New Jersey, Thomas Nelson & Sons, 1967.

Richardson, Brenda, cataloguer, *Jugendstil & Expressionism in German Posters. An Exhibition Organized by Herschel B. Chipp*. Berkeley, California, Pasadena Art Museum, The University of California, 1965.

Schmutzler, Robert, *Art Nouveau*. New York, Harry N. Abrams, Inc., 1964.

Selz, Peter and Constantine, Mildred, eds., *Art Nouveau: Art and Design at the Turn of the Century*. New York, The Museum of Modern Art, 1959.

Notes

IDENTIFYING ART NOUVEAU

1. Robert Schmutzler, *Art Nouveau* (New York, Harry N. Abrams, Inc., 1964), p. 274.

2. Stephan Tschudi Madsden, *Sources of Art Nouveau* (New York, George Wittenborn, 1955).

3. Peter Selz and Mildred Constantine, eds., *Art Nouveau: Art and Design at the Turn of the Century* (New York, The Museum of Modern Art, 1959), p. 12.

4. Nikolaus Pevsner, *The Sources of Modern Architecture and Design* (New York, Frederick A. Praeger, Publishers, 1968), p. 66.

ART NOUVEAU GLASS

1. Albert Christian Revi, *American Art Nouveau Glass* (New Jersey, Thomas Nelson & Sons 1968), p. 24.

2 & 3. William Ernest Mouser, Jr., and Peggy Joyce Gurn, *Cristal d'Emile Gallé: Only a King Would Buy* (Privately printed, copyright 1966 by William Ernest Mouser, Jr., and Peggy Joyce Gurn), pp. 12, 18, 30.

4. Ray and Lee Grover, *Art Glass Nouveau* (Vermont, Charles E. Tuttle Company, 1967), p. 65.

ART NOUVEAU POTTERY

1. Henry Winter, *The Dynasty of Louis Comfort Tiffany* (South Hanover, Massachusetts, privately printed,), pp. 57–70.

2. Dorothy McGraw Bogue, *The Van Briggle Story* (Colorado Springs, Colorado, privately printed, 1968), p. 43.

3. Louise and Evan Purviance and Norris F. Schneider *Zanesville Art Pottery in Color* (Iowa, Mid-America Book Company, 1968), p. 11.

ART NOUVEAU JEWELRY

1. Philip Wilson, ed., *Art at Auction: The Year at Sotheby's & Parke-Bernet, 1966–1967* (New York, American Heritage Publishing Company, Inc., 1967), p. 231.

ART NOUVEAU FURNITURE

1. Pevsner, *op. cit.*, p. 80.

2. Selz, *op. cit.*, p. 92.

GRAPHIC ARTS AND SCULPTURE

1. Selz, *op. cit.*, p. 87.

Index

Aesthetic Movement, The: Prelude to
  Art Nouveau (Aslin), 199
Albert Brothers, 106, 139
Aldin, Cecil C. W., 67
Alvin Mfg. Co., 99, 100
American Art Nouveau Glass (Revi), 34, 36, 51
American Silver Company, 100
American Spoons (Rainwater and Felger), 106
Angst, Albert, 191
Ansonia clocks, 111, 113
Antique Trader Price Guide to Antiques
  & Collectors' Objects (Mebane), 246
Antiques (magazine), 245
Antiques Journal, The, 41, 95, 245
Architectural glass, 44
Architecture, 26, 209
Art at Auction (Wilson), 75
Art Glass Nouveau (Grover), 48
Art Nouveau (Schmutzler), 17, 199
Art Nouveau: Art and Design at the
  Turn of the Century (Selz and
  Constantine, eds.), 19, 79
Arts and Crafts movement, 22
Ashbee, Charles Robert, 77, 101
Ashtrays, 56, 98, 103, 137, 139
Aslin, Elizabeth, 199
Associated Artists, 30, 188
Auction sales, 241–43
Aurene glass, 46, 225

Baby: rattles, 129, 131; spoons, 106
Bach, Martin, 45
Bach, Martin, Jr., 45
Bag checks, 108, 145
Baking dishes, 161
Barbour Silver Plate Co., 165, 175
Barrettes, 11, 87, 121, 122
Bayer, Ralph E., 64
Beardsley, Aubrey, 11, 18, 19, 24, 199–201
Beaux-Arts Exposition of 1904, 191
Becken Company, A. C., 122
Behrens, Peter, 24, 203
Benedict Mfg. Co., M. S., 103
Benson, W. A. S., 101
Berlage, Hendrik Petrus, 188
Berlin Museum, 42
Berry bowls, 163
Bethnal Green Museum, 183, 186
Bienvenu, Ferdinand, 191
Bindesbøll, Thorvald, 103
Bing, Marcel, 77
Bing, Samuel, 17, 18, 31
Birch, William, 194
Bird, E. B., 205
Birth spoons, 106
Blackington & Company, R., 100
Blake, William, 20, 197
Blotters, 149, 153, 155
Bogue, Dorothy McGraw, 62

Bonbon dishes: pottery, 66; silver, 98,
  132, 167; scoops, 132
Bonnard, Pierre, 18
Book binding, 26
Book covers, 203
Book marks, 108, 155–56
Book of Rookwood Pottery, The (Peck), 61
Bookplates, 203
Bottle: corks, 145; openers, 99, 145
Bottles: scent, 44; unguent, 44
Bourdet, Eugene, 191
Boudoir accessories, 44, 121, 233
Bowls: glass, 40; pottery, 56, 62, 66;
  silver, 97
Boxes, 11, 38, 56, 108
Bradley, William H., 18, 26, 201, 204, 208
Brides' baskets, 163, 234
Brushes, 98, 107, 108, 126
Buffalo Pottery, 67–69, 226
Bugati, Charles, 191
Burne-Jones, Sir Edward, 199
Button hooks, 98, 126

Cake baskets, 167
Cameo glass, 34, 38, 40, 41, 42, 48,
  217–19, 222–24, 225
Cambridge Art Pottery, 230
Candelabra, 102, 173–77
Candlesticks: pottery, 60, 66; silver,
  95, 97, 98, 102, 103, 173–77
Cane heads, 108, 143
Card cases, 98, 129
Carder, Frederick, 29, 46
Carnival glass, 46
Carqueville, Will, 205
Carson Pirie Scott & Company, 192
Caster sets, 163, 165, 234–35
Causee, J., 208
Cellini, Benvenuto, 77
Celluloid, 87, 122, 145
Centerpieces, 161
Century Guild Hobby Horse, The, 24
Century Magazine, 204
Chap-Book, The, 203, 204, 205, 208
Charms. See Watch charms
Charpentier, Alexandre, 186
Chatelaine: chains, 118; puff boxes,
  131; purses, 121
Chez de Stape, 75
Chicago Auditorium, 26
Chicago World's Fair, 31
Chocolate pots, 60
Christie's (auction), 13
Cigar: containers, 11; cutters, 141;
  jars, 135–36; lighters, 95, 97
Cigarette cases, 98, 108, 139; paper cases, 139
Cincinnati Art Museum, 60
Cincinnati Artistic Wrought Iron Works, 51
Cire perdue casting, 44

Clock cases, 66
Clocks, 103, 111–16, 232–33
Coats-Connelly col. of Tiffany glass, 10, 29
Codman, William J., 93
Cohen, Hal L., 246
Coleman, Samuel, 30
Collector's Weekly, 245
Colonna, Eugène, 77, 188
Combe, William, 69
Combs, 108, 121, 122, 126, 145
Community Silver Company, 100
Complete Antiques Price List, The (Kovel), 246
Condiment sets, 11
Constant, Benjamin, 61
Continental Mfg. Co., 192
Copenhagen pottery, 70
Corkscrews, 145
Costume accessories, 79
Coty perfumers, 42
Court plaster cases, 11, 108
Cranach, William Lucas von, 79
Cranch, E. P., 60
Crane, Walter, 197
Craythorne, William, 102
Cream and sugar sets, 102
Crescent watches, 116
Cristallerie de Pantin, 48
Cruet sets, 163, 234–35
Crumb sets, 107
Curling irons, 108
Cypriote glass, 34

Daniel, Greta, 79, 188, 201
Daum Nancy glass, 48, 218–19
Décorchemont, François, 48
De Feure, Georges, 188
D'Ernys, Mme., 191
Delatte glass, 219
Dent, John, 199
Desbois, Jules, 77
DeVez glass, 48
Dial, 24
Dr. Syntax's Three Tours (Combe), 69
Dominick & Haff, 99
Donahue, Dr. and Mrs. Walter, 48
Dresser, Christopher, 69
Dubois, Paul, 79
Dufrène, Maurice, 77, 191
Durand, Victor, 29, 45, 219–20
Durgin, William B., 99; Company, 99

Eckmann, Otto, 24, 203
Ecole de Nancy, 186, 187
Ehrström, Eric, 103
Elkintons, 101
Ellmore Silver Company, 99
Elvira Studio, 24
Enameled glass, 38, 40, 44
Endell, August, 24
Envelope racks, 108, 158
Epergnes, 161
Eyeglass holders, 108, 129

Fabergé, Peter Carl, 73
Face powder books, 132
Favrile: glass, 31–37, 46, 216–17;
    pottery, 55–56
Felger, Donna H., 107
Fenton Art Glass Company, 46
Fern, Alan M., 19
Fern dishes, 108, 169
Figurines, 44
Fisher, Katie, 77
Flasks, pocket, 99, 135, 143
Follet, Paul, 77
Forbes Silver Company, 107, 170
Ford, Johnson & Company, J.S., 192
Foster & Brother Co., Theodore W., 100
Fostoria Glass Specialty Company, 46
Fouquet, Georges, 77
Frames, picture, 98, 103, 108
Frankel Light Company, 51
Fruit dishes, 44, 161, 163, 234
Fry, Laura A., 60
Fuller, Löie, 207–8, 243
Furniture, 26, 181–94, 236

Gaillard, Claude Ferdinand, 188
Gallé, Emile, 10, 11, 18, 24, 31, 38–42,
    56–58, 183, 217–18, 226
Gallery of Modern Art, 200
Garter buckles, 131
Gaskin, Mr. and Mrs. Arthur, 77
Gaudí, Antonio, 12, 19, 188, 207
Gauguin, Paul, 197
Gentil, Alphonse, 191
Gilbert, Albert, 24
Gilbert Clock Company, 111, 113, 114
Glasgow School of Art, 24, 186, 187
Glasgow School style, 187, 188
Glass, 26, 29–51, 215–25. *See also*
    individual factories and craftsmen
Glove stretchers, 126
Gorham Mfg. Co., 93–97, 99, 173
Graphic arts, 197–207, 237
Grasset, Eugène, 18, 77
Gregory, Anne (Mrs. Artus Van
    Briggle), 61
Grover, Ray and Lee, 48
Guaranty Building (Buffalo), 192
Guerinet, Armand, 191
Guild and School of Handicraft, 77
Guimard, Hector, 12, 19, 24, 186, 207
Gurn, Peggy Joyce, 40, 41

Hair accessories: curlers, 126; pins,
    122; receivers, 11, 108
Hamburg Museum, 42
Handel & Company, 46, 220
Hand-painted porcelain, 168
Hatpin holders, 108, 124
Hatpins, 11, 82, 86, 108, 124
Hazenflug, Frank, 201, 205
Hem gauges, 132
Henry, J. S., 194
Herring, Lois B., 45

Herschede Hall Clock Company, 58
Hirsch & Company, A., 169
Historicism, 17
Hobbies, 245
Hodgkinson, Ethel M., 77
Hodgkinson, Winifred, 77
Hodler, Ferdinand, 204
Hoffmann, Josef, 26, 103
Hofmann, Ludwig von, 203, 204
Homan Mfg. Co., 99, 163
Homan Silver Plate Company, 152,
 165, 167, 169, 175
Horta, Victor, 11, 22, 188
House of Pomegranates, A, 203
Hubbard, Clarence T., 45
Hubbard, Elbert, 67
Hutton & Sons, W., 101

Ice buckets and pails, 168
Imperial Glass Company, 46, 220
Initial letters, 207
Ink stands, 11, 149, 152, 204
Inkwells, 56
Inland Printer, The, 204
International Silver Company, 107

Japanese influence on style, 20, 38, 69,
 197, 199, 205
Jardinieres, 36, 56, 66
Jennings Bros. Mfg. Co., 113
Jewelers' Circular-Weekly, The, 95
Jewelry, 11, 26, 73–89, 231–32
Jewel: boxes, 44, 66, 102, 107, 126; trees, 108
Jugend, 24, 203
Jugendstil, 12, 17, 18, 24, 69, 188, 203

Kensington Museum, 42
Kew Blas glass, 45, 220–21
Key accessories: rings, 145; tags, 145
Klinger, Max, 203
Klimdt, Gustav, 26, 203, 204
Knives, pocket, 135, 145
Knox, Alexander, 102
Knox, Archibald, 77
Kovel, Ralph and Terry, 246

Laeuger, Max, 69
Lalique, Marc, 44, 45
Lalique, Maria-Claude, 45
Lalique, René 10, 11, 18, 24, 42–44,
 73–77; et Cie, 42, 221–22
Lamp: Gallé, 41; Handel, 46, 220;
 Rookwood, 60; Tiffany, 29, 33–34,
 36, 55, 215–16
Lancelot and the Ladies (Bradley), 204
Laporte, Léo, 208
Larche, Raoul, 208
Larcombe, E., 77
Larkin Company, 67
L'Art Décoratif, 203
Lava glass, 34
Laurelton Hall, 56
La Verre Français glass, 48, 222

Legras, August J. F., 48
Legras glass, 48, 222–23
Léonard, Agathon, 209
Letter openers, 11, 108, 129, 155
Léveillé, E. B., 48
Levin, Hugo, 103
Libbey Glass Company, 48
Liberty and Company, 102, 194
Lighting fixtures, 44
Linthorpe Pottery, 69
Lithographs, 203, 237
Loetz glass, 51, 223
Long, W. A., 64
Lonhuda Pottery, 60, 64
Lorgnettes, 99, 129; holders, 129
Low & Company, Daniel, 99
Lustre Art Glass Company, 45
Luxembourg Museum, 42
Lysistrata, 200

Macdonald, Frances, 24, 102, 188, 203
Macdonald, Margaret, 24, 102, 188, 203
Mackintosh, Charles Rennie, 10, 24,
 102, 186–88, 236
Mackmurdo, Arthur H., 24, 188
Madsen, Stephan Tschudi, 22
Maillol, Aristide, 207
Maison de l'Art Nouveau, 17
Maison du Peuple, 22
Majorelle, Louis, 24, 186, 191
Mallory, Thomas, 199
Manicure accessories, 98, 108, 121, 126, 145
Martelé silver, 93–97, 173, 177
Martin brothers, 69
Match safes, 98, 108, 135, 139
Mauser Manufacturing Company, 99
McClinton, Katharine Morrison, 95
McLeish, Annie, 77
McNair, Frances, 77
McNair, J. Herbert, 77
Meissen porcelain, 70
Memo tablets, 132
Metropolitan Museum of Art, 207
Millefiori glass, 34
Minne, Georges, 207
Minton pottery, 70
Mirrors, 98, 108, 121, 126, 131
Modernismo, 17
Mont Joy glass, 48
Month spoons, 106
Morris, Talwyn, 77
Morris, William, 20, 22, 101, 197
Morte d'Arthur (Mallory), 199
Moser, Kolomon, 26
Mt. Vernon Company Silversmiths, 99
Mt. Washington Glass Company, 48
Mouser, William Ernest, Jr. 40, 41
Mugs: pottery, 66; silver, 108, 169
Müller, Albin, 103
Muller Frères, 48, 223
Munch, Edvard, 18, 26, 203
Musée des Arts Décoratifs, 42, 186, 208
Museum of Modern Art, 12, 186

Nabis, 203
Napkin rings, 11, 99, 103, 107
Nash, A. Douglas, 33, 37; Corporation, 37, 45, 223–24
Nash, Arthur J., 33
Nash, Leslie H., 33
National Antiques Review, 245
New England Glass Company, 48
New England Watch Company, 116
New Haven Clock Company, 113
New York Public Library Art Department, 207
Nichols, Mrs. Maria Longworth, 58, 61
Nineteenth Century Glass: Its Genesis and Development (Revi), 105
Novelties: pottery, 66; silver, 99, 105
Nut bowls, 108, 163

Obrist, Hermann, 24, 207
Official Price Guide to Antiques, Curios, 246
Olbrich, Josef, 26, 103
Old Hickory Chair Company, 194
Oskamp, Nolting & Company, 139
Owens Pottery Co., J. B., 64, 66, 226

Paintings, 197, 201, 204, 236
Paling stijl, 17
Pan, 24, 203
Pankok, Bernhard, 24
Pantin glass, 48
Paper adjuncts: creasers, 98; cutters, 98, 103, 129, 155; racks, 158
Paris International Exposition of 1900, 26
Paris Exposition, 1889, 31
Paris Metro, 19, 207
Parke-Bernet Galleries, 10, 13, 29, 56
Pasadena Art Museum, 12,
Pâte-sur-pâte technique, 70
Paye & Baker, 100
Pencils, 149; cases, 108
Pens, 152–53; holders, 152; racks, 152; trays, 108
Peter Poodle, 204
Peters Company, H. J., 51
Pevsner, Nikolaus, 12, 26
Phoenix glass, 224
Pickard, Inc., 230
Pickett, Edith, 77
Pincushions, 98, 129
Pioneers of Modern Design from William Morris to Walter Gropius (Pevsner), 12
Pipes, 11, 135, 141
Pitchers: pottery, 66, 67; silver, 95
Pogačnik, Theodor, 103
Pomona glass, 48
Pope, Alexander, 200
Postal card holders, 158
Posters, 24, 26, 203, 204, 205–7, 237
Price guides, 245–46
Prices, 213–37
Prouvé, Victor, 77, 186

Puff jars, 11, 108, 126
Purdy, Ross C., 66
Purses, 108
Purviance, Louise and Evan, 66
Pyrtz, Torolf, 103

Quezal Art Glass & Decorating Company, 45

Rainwater, Dorothy T., 107
Raguel, Auguste, 191
Ramsden, Omar, 101
Rape of the Lock, The (Pope), 200
Razor strops, 143
Reed, Ethel, 201, 205
Reed & Barton, 93, 99, 100, 152, 170, 175
Revi, Albert Christian, 32, 33, 34, 36, 45, 51
Rhead, Louis, 205
Richard, Paul, 77
Ricketts, Charles, 24, 203
Riemerschmid, Richard, 102, 188
Rivaud, Charles, 77
Robin Hood (Rhead), 205
Robinson, Fred, 77
Roche, Pierre, 208
Rogers & Bro., 100
Rogers & Son, William, 100
Rogers, William A., 100, 161
Rogers, William B., 100
Romance of the Road Ahead, The, 67
Rookwood Pottery, 10, 55, 58–61, 226–27
Rosetti, Dante Gabriel, 197
Roseville pottery, 10, 64, 66, 227
Rothschild Department Store, 26, 192
Rousseau, Eugène, 48
Rowlandson, Thomas, 69
Roxenburg pottery, 70
Royal Bayreuth ceramics, 230
Royal Bonn, 111
Royal Doulton, 70, 227–28
Roycroft Corporation, 67
R. S. Prussia porcelain, 230

St. Petersburg Museum, 42
Salome (Wilde), 200
Salon de l'Art Nouveau, 18
Salon des Artistes Française, 75
Sauvage and Sazarin, 191
Savoy, The, 200
Scharvogel, Johann J., 69
Schmutzler, Robert, 17, 20, 199
Schneider, Norris F., 66
School and Guild of Handicraft, 101
Scissors, 98, 108
Sculpture, 207–9, 237
Seals, wax, 156
Secessionsstil, 17, 69
Sechrist Manufacturing Company, Albert, 51
Segantini, G., 203
Selz, Peter, 19, 22
Sevres porcelain, 70, 229–30
Shades, light, 33

Shaving accessories: brushes, 11, 141; mugs, 141, 143; sets, 108, 143; soap boxes and cups, 141
Shirayamadani, Kataro, 60
Shoe horns, 98, 126
Sicard, Jacques, 64
Silver, 93–108, 232; plated, 99–101, 232. *See also* individual manufacturers
Silver-deposit ware, 103, 224
Simpson, Edgar, 77
Simpson, Hall, Miller & Co., 108, 149, 153, 161, 163, 165, 168, 169, 175
Sloan, John, 205
Solon, Leon Victor, 70
Solon, M. L., 70
Sotheby's, 13, 75
Southall Pottery, 69
Souvenir spoons, 11, 102, 105–7, 232
Spaulding & Company, 97
Spinning Wheel, 45, 245
Spoils, 204
Starr, Theodore B., 97
Sterling Company, 99
Steuben glass, 45, 224–25
Stevens and Williams, 48
Stile floreale, 17
Stile liberty, 17
Stourbridge Glass Company, 32, 33
Studio, 199, 203
Style des Vingt, le, 17
Sullivan, Louis, 12, 26, 192
Suspenders, 145
Susse Frères Foundry, 209

Table accessories, 161–70
Tape measures, 132
Tassel House, 22
Tea caddies, 108
Teapots, 60, 102
Teplitz ceramics, 229
Thayer & Chandler, 169
Thimble cases, 132
Thomas clocks, Seth, 113, 114
Tie clasps, 145
Tiffany, Charles L., 30
Tiffany, Louis Comfort, 10, 11, 12, 18, 26, 29–38, 188; Furnaces, 32, 33, 37
Tiffany & Company, 30, 36, 56
Tiffany Glass Company, 30
Tiffany Glass & Decorating Co., 31
Tiffany glass prices, 215–17
Tiffany Studios, 31, 32, 36, 38
Tiles, 56
Title pages, 203, 207
Toilet articles, 121, 126
Toorop, Jan, 26, 203, 204
Tooth: brush bottles, 11, 126; brushes, 98, 126
Tortoise shell, 122
Toulouse-Lautrec, Henri de, 18, 24, 197, 205, 208
Trays: bread, 165; dresser, 44, 98, 108

Umbrella heads, 145

Unger Brothers, 93, 97–98, 124, 126, 129, 131, 137, 143, 155, 175, 177
Union Glass Company, 45
U.S. Art Bent Glass Company, 51

Valentien, Albert B., 60
Valentien, Anna Marie, 60
Vallotton, Felix, 201
Val St. Lambert, 51
Van Briggle, Artus, 10, 60, 61, 62; Company, 62; Pottery, 61–63, 228
Van de Velde, Henri, 11, 22, 79, 102, 188, 203, 204
Vanity cases, 98, 132
Vases: glass, 29, 34–37, 46; pottery, 55, 60
Veazey, David, 77
Venus and Tannehauser (Beardsley illus.), 200
Ver Sacrum, 203
Vever, M., 77
Victor Bicycle Company, 204
Victoria & Albert Museum, 42, 102, 200
Vineland Flint Glass Works, 45
Voysey, Charles Annesley, 24, 188

Wagner, Otto, 26
Wallace & Sons Mfg. Co., R., 93, 100
Wallenstein, Mayer & Co., 106, 141, 165
Wallets, 145
Waltham watches, 116
Walton, George, 187
Warman, E. G., 246
Warman's Antiques and Their Current Prices (Warman), 246
Watches, 116–17, 233; chains, 86, 117; charms, 188; fobs, 86, 117
Waterbury Clock Company, 113, 114
Waterman Company, A. A., 153
Water sets, 167
Wayside Press, 204
Webb & Sons, Thomas, 48, 225
Webster & Sons, E. G., 99, 165
Wedgwood, Josiah, 156
Weller, Samuel A., 64; Pottery, 10, 64, 228–29
Western Clock Company, 113, 114
Western Collector, 64, 245
Wheeler, Candace, 30
Whistler, James McNeill, 197
Whiting & Company, F. M., 99
Wilde, Oscar, 24, 199
Wine coolers, 168
Witwe, J. Löetz, 51
Wolfers, Philip, 79
Women's Art Museum Association (Cincinnati), 60
Wonderbox Stories, The (Bradley), 204
Woodcuts, 203
Woodside Sterling Company, 99
Writing accessories, 149–58, 234

Yellow Book, The, 200
Young & Company, Otto, 106, 107, 131, 156

Zanesville Art Pottery (Schneider), 66